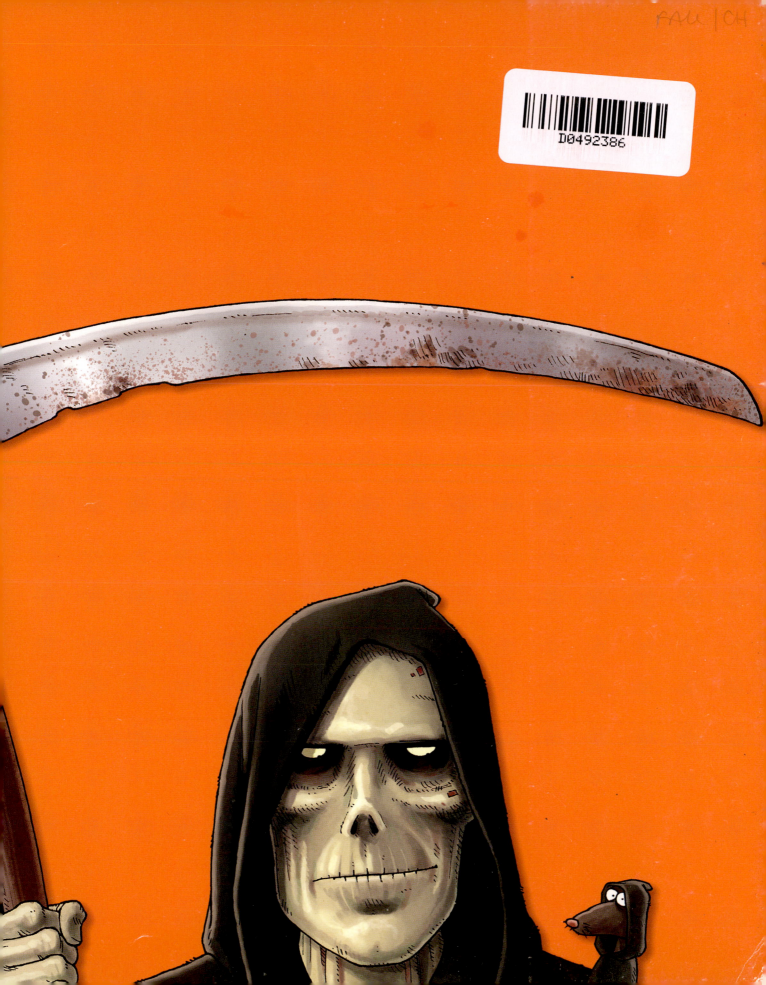

DEADLY DAYS in HISTORY

Terry Deary

Illustrated by
Martin Brown

■SCHOLASTIC

**This book is dedicated to the memory of Adam Littlejohns of Burnhope –
a true fan and a sad loss. TD**

**To Alyx Price and her marvellous team (and dinners after the events).
Huge thanks. MB**

www.horrible-histories.co.uk
www.terry-deary.com

Scholastic Children's Books,
Euston House, 24 Eversholt Street,
London NW1 1DB, UK

A division of Scholastic Ltd
London ~ New York ~ Toronto ~ Sydney ~ Auckland
Mexico City ~ New Delhi ~ Hong Kong

Editorial Project Manager: Jill Sawyer
Assistant Editor: Corinne Lucas

First published in the UK by Scholastic Ltd, 2013
This edition published 2014

Text copyright © Terry Deary, 2013
Illustration copyright © Martin Brown, 2013
Colour by Rob Davis

All rights reserved

ISBN 978 1407 12146 8

Printed and bound by Tien Wah Press Pte. Ltd, Malaysia

2 4 6 8 10 9 7 5 3 1

CONTENTS

BLACK DEATH STRIKES,
CAFFA CITY, 1347 **34**

BATTLE OF CRÉCY,
NORTHERN FRANCE, 26 AUGUST 1346 **36**

DEATH OF JOAN OF ARC,
FRANCE, 14TH MAY 1431 **38**

BATTLE OF TOWTON,
ENGLAND, 29 MARCH 1461 **40**

CHRISTOPHER COLUMBUS SETS OFF FOR
AMERICA, 3 AUGUST 1492 **42**

LUTHER AND THE CHURCH DOOR,
GERMANY, 31 OCTOBER 1517 **44**

FERDINAND MAGELLAN SAILS THE WORLD,
20 SEPTEMBER 1519 **45**

DESTRUCTION OF AZTECS,
MEXICO, 16 MAY 1521 **46**

ST BARTHOLOMEW'S DAY MASSACRE, PARIS,
FRANCE, 23 AUGUST 1572 **48**

SPANISH ARMADA,
ENGLISH CHANNEL, 19 JULY 1588 **50**

VIRGINIA SETTLERS LAND,
NORTH AMERICA, MAY 1607 **52**

PILGRIM FATHERS REACH
AMERICA, 21 DECEMBER 1620 **54**

BUNKER HILL BATTLE,
AMERICA, 17 JUNE 1775 **56**

DEATH OF CAPTAIN COOK,
PACIFIC OCEAN, 14 FEBRUARY 1779 **58**

FIRST CONVICT SHIPS SAIL TO
AUSTRALIA, 13 MAY 1787 **59**

THE END OF THE TERROR IN THE FRENCH
REVOLUTION, PARIS, 27 JULY 1794 **60**

A BAN ON NEW SLAVES,
AMERICA, MARCH 3 1807 **62**

RAINHILL TRAIN ACCIDENT,
ENGLAND, 15 SEPTEMBER 1830 **64**

INTRODUCTION

History has been around for nearly 5,000 years. Before that we say it's 'prehistoric' ... you know, stone-agers hunting all day with wooden spears and coming home to caves with no television.

Then, 2,500 years ago, the first real history books were written by an ancient Greek called Herodotus. He gathered all the facts about the past, checked them and put them in order. He got the name 'Father of History'.

I'M THE DADDY

But even Herodotus couldn't tell every story of what every person did every day in history. It would be a book as tall as a mountain and it would be very, very boring.

He just picked the big, BIG, B-I-G bits. The events that changed the world.

All historians do that. But Horrible Histories pick the bits that are B-I-G and HORRIBLE. The dreadful days of death, disease, danger and dancing. (Yes. Dancing.)

Even a horrible history of the world would make such a big book we would use all the wood in the world to print it ... and we'd all die of Dutch Elm disease. (With no elms to eat the Dutch Elm beetles would start eating us instead.)

KILL

We can't have that. What we need is a book that tells you only the top 50 of the filthy and foul facts.

Seventy-two Horrible Historians worked day and night for 18 years to read a pile of history books as tall as the Eiffel Tower. They chose the best of the best.

What happened to them, you ask? Tragedy.

When the pile of books blew over they were all crushed (horribly). Luckily they had just finished this book ... well, not so lucky for the 72 horrible historians, but lucky for you.

Read on ...

IF YOU DARE!

THE FIRST MASSACRE, TALHEIM

History has always been horrible. It seems that humans have been killing other humans forever.

There are ancient graves showing skeletons of humans who died with chopped bodies and smashed skulls. Those hacked humans died 34,000 years ago. So, Horrible History has seen at least 34,000 years of murder and misery.

In 1983, a man in Talheim, Germany, went out to his garden to dig up a cabbage for lunch and found human bones. (That is enough to put you off your Sunday dinner.)

The police were called. They dug and found hundreds of bones. Was the cabbage man a serial killer … had he killed cornflakes for breakfast? (Was he a cereal killer?)

No. Doctors said the bones were 7,000 years old. Police said it was too late to catch the killers.

Then the archaeologists had a look and found 34 skeletons…

SIXTEEN CHILDREN AND SEVEN WOMEN — JUST NINE MEN … SO THEY WEREN'T A WAR GROUP..

SEE THESE SKULLS? EIGHTEEN OF THEM HAVE HOLES IN THE BACK OR THE TOP. THEY WERE TRYING TO RUN AWAY

THREE HAVE BEEN SHOT. SEE THE BONES HAVE ARROW SCRAPES?

MAYBE IT WAS A BAND OF HUNTERS THAT UPSET A BAND OF FARMERS. MAYBE THE KILLERS WERE CANNIBALS — THE LOSERS WERE EATEN BY THE WINNERS!

I NEVER DID GET TO PULL UP THAT CABBAGE

In Herxheim, Germany, an ancient grave was full of people massacred for another popular reason – religion. The Herxheim heads had been chopped off and stuck up high on poles.

An early sacrifice to the gods. Gods cause an awful lot of trouble.

EGYPT, 2566 BC
THE BIGGEST PYRAMID

The Egyptians were a bit funny when it came to funerals. They built the awesome pyramids to bury their kings in.

In 2566 BC, the Egyptian King Khufu died. He wanted to be remembered for a very, v-e-r-y long time. So he had the world's biggest pyramid built … and then wasn't buried in it. Where is his body? It's a mystery.

Khufu is remembered for building that pyramid but he is also said to have been super-cruel.

TOP TIPS – HOW TO BE REMEMBERED FOREVER … BE CRUEL AS KHUFU

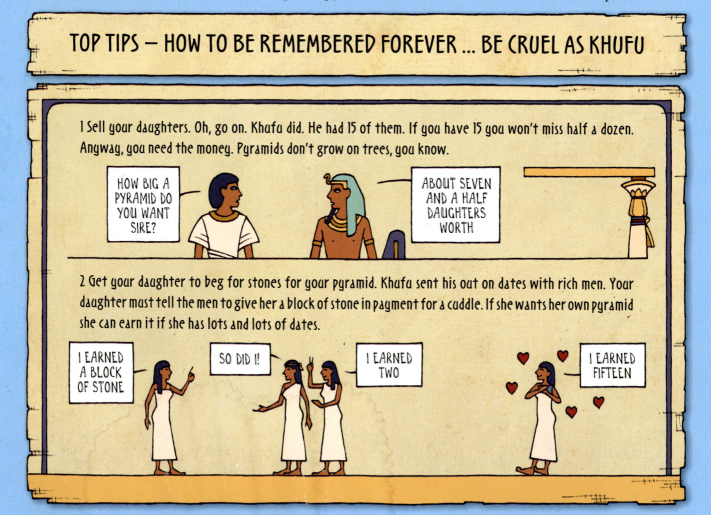

3 Bully your peasants. Tell your peasants they have to build you a pyramid with over two million blocks. They will end up with twisted bodies and die. Do you care? No.

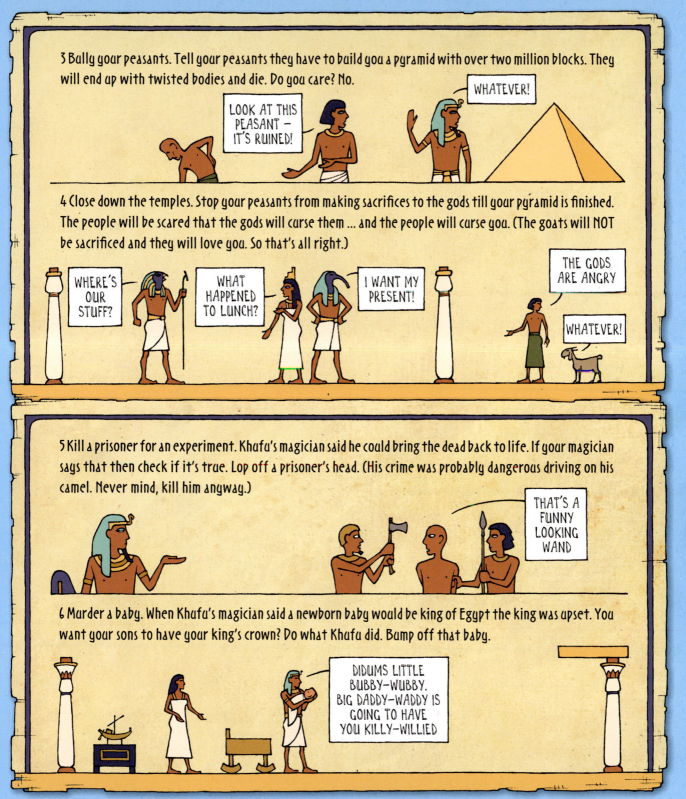

4 Close down the temples. Stop your peasants from making sacrifices to the gods till your pyramid is finished. The people will be scared that the gods will curse them ... and the people will curse you. (The goats will NOT be sacrificed and they will love you. So that's all right.)

5 Kill a prisoner for an experiment. Khufu's magician said he could bring the dead back to life. If your magician says that then check if it's true. Lop off a prisoner's head. (His crime was probably dangerous driving on his camel. Never mind, kill him anyway.)

6 Murder a baby. When Khufu's magician said a newborn baby would be king of Egypt the king was upset. You want your sons to have your king's crown? Do what Khufu did. Bump off that baby.

Kruel Khufu. But at least he was nice to his mother and built her a pyramid all of her own. Remember, if you're a king of Egypt ALWAYS be nice to your mummy.

OLYMPUS, GREECE, 776 BC
FIRST OLYMPIC GAMES

The ancient Greeks enjoyed games. Their cities battled against each other for prizes. The first Olympic Games were probably held in 776 BC ... and they could become quite gory games. If you want to run a REAL Olympics here are the rules...

OLYMPIC RULES

1 Naked men only. Women and girls are banned. They can't even watch.

2 Women who sneak in will be executed by throwing off a cliff. Don't even think about it, girls.

3 There are running, jumping and throwing contests. Relay races with flaming torches. A sports arena is one 'stadion' long (190 metres).

4 There is chariot racing as well as music, speaking and theatre contests for the not−so−fit.

5 Winners get crowns made from wild olive branches.

6 The winners at the Isthmian games are given a crown of CELERY as a prize.

7 The winner's name will also be called out to the crowds. You'll be famous.

8 Winners get free meals for life and pay no more taxes ... ever.

9 In 'pancration' wrestling you can strangle, kick, twist and even jump up and down on your opponent. How much fun is that?

10 Cheats will be fined — you have to buy an expensive statue to the god Zeus. So cut out the cons.

Those four-horse chariot races could be deadly dangerous. The poet, Homer, described an accident ...

> *Eumelos was thrown out of the chariot beside the wheel. The skin was ripped from the elbows, nose and mouth, and his forehead smashed in over the eyebrows. His eyes filled with tears and his powerful voice was silenced.*

The modern Olympics aren't so much fun.

GREECE, 480 BC

BATTLE OF THERMOPYLAE

The mighty Greeks fought the powerful Persians to see who ruled the world. The Persians marched towards Greece. King Leonidas of Greece led a little Spartan army against a hundred thousand Persians. If you were Leonidas, what would YOU do? Surrender if you had any sense. What did Loony Leonidas do? He decided to try to stop the Persians at the narrow pass of Thermopylae. He couldn't win. Brave? Or batty?

The Persians sent a messenger…   Leonidas sent the famous reply…

> YOU CANNOT WIN, LEONIDAS BUT WE WILL SPARE YOU. LAY DOWN YOUR WEAPONS

> COME AND GET THEM!

✤ The Persians came and got them. The story says a little army of 300 Spartans and 2,000 Greeks held back the Persian army for two days.

✤ Then a Greek traitor showed the Persians a way around the pass to attack Leonidas from behind.

✤ On the third day the Persians won.

✤ 2,000 Greeks and Spartans lay dead … but 20,000 Persians had been killed.

✤ A gravestone on the Spartan burial pit says to anyone reading it…

> STRANGER, GO TELL THE SPARTANS THAT WE LIE HERE TRUE TO OUR SPARTAN WAY OF LIFE, EVEN TO THE DEATH

It doesn't say, 'The Persians won so it was a pretty daft way to die.'

☠ FOUL FACT ☠

The Persian winners cut the head off Leonidas's body. The corpse was crucified. His bones were finally taken back to Sparta to be buried 40 years after the battle.

SOUTHERN ITALY, 280 BC
BATTLE OF HERACLEA

You can win a battle with a lot of savage slaughter. But that doesn't always win you the whole war. We call that sort of win a 'Pyrrhic Victory'. Why? It is named after King Pyrrhus.

In 280 BC, Pyrrhus of Epirus invaded the Roman lands. The Roman army set off to fight him.

Pyrrhus was worried that the Romans might try to kill him first. So what did the crafty king do? He swapped armour with his bodyguard. The poor bodyguard was killed and the Romans cheered. Then Pyrrhus took off his helmet, rode forward and cried…

✹ Pyrrhus brought his battle elephants forward and the Romans were smashed and massacred … smashacred in fact.

✹ BOTH sides lost around 15,000 men. But the Romans got new soldiers from Rome. Pyrrhus was a long way from home and his army was shrunk. His famous words after the battle were…

✠ FAST FACT ✠

Pyrrhus had a doctor who slipped across to the Roman camp and said:

The Romans were shocked at this sneaky way of winning. They were such good sports they TOLD Pyrrhus of the doctor's plan. Pyrrhus lived on. The doctor didn't.

THE ALPS, 218 BC
HANNIBAL'S ELEPHANT ATTACK

The rotten Romans met a new enemy, the city of Carthage, North Africa. The Carthage leader was called Hannibal and he made one of history's most famously fearless trips.

The Romans were just about to set out to attack Carthage when they got shock news…

HAN HAS A DIFFERENT PLAN. HE HAS LANDED IN SPAIN SO HE CAN ATTACK US FROM THE NORTH

ALPS

PYRENEES

ROME

CARTHAGE

The clever Romans said Han was a mad man. He could NOT cross the huge mountains (the Pyrenees and the Alps) and get to Rome. Could he? Hannibal set off with 40 war elephants and 40,000 soldiers.

After a terrible two-week trip he was left with just four elephants. Yes, that's 36 elephants dead on the road. (10,000 soldiers died too but they asked for it—the elephants didn't.) Still, Hannibal reached Italy and smashed the Romans.

Han was a wicked victor. He made his Roman prisoners fight one another to the death. The winner would go free. This was to teach his own soldiers of Carthage that death in a fight is better than death as a prisoner. Then one day he had a bright idea…

YOU, ROMAN PRISONER, WILL FIGHT TO THE DEATH AGAINST AN ELEPHANT

ERR…!

BUT WHEN THE PRISONER FOUGHT…

I WIN! SET ME FREE

HANNIBAL WAS FURIOUS...

IF THE ROMANS EVER HEAR HOW EASY IT IS TO KILL ELEPHANTS WE'RE FINISHED!

I CAN'T SET YOU FREE. WE'LL KILL YOU ANYWAY!

BUT I WON!!!

But in the end, Hannibal was defeated. He went into exile and swallowed poison so the Romans couldn't capture him. Years later, the Romans won the last Carthage War. They captured Carthage and massacred many of the people. The Roman general, Scipio, gave the order to kill everyone they met.

The soldiers did more than that – the Romans…

✱ beheaded men.
✱ threw babies into fires.
✱ cut women open so their guts spilled out.
✱ cut the legs off animals and chopped the dogs in two.

As the city burned the people hiding in the cellars roasted. The ones hiding upstairs threw themselves to their deaths in the streets below.

☠ FAST FACTS ☠

There was always a danger Hannibal's elephants would panic and charge their own soldiers. So the riders had a jumbo spike and a hammer. If an elephant started attacking his friends, the driver would hammer the spike into the elephant's brain to stop it. The armies of Carthage used North African Elephants. They are now extinct. Are you surprised?

thirty nine thousand nine hundred and ninety nine men

OUCH!

Germany, AD 9

BATTLE OF TEUTOBURGER FOREST

The Roman legions marched across the world and beat the natives wherever they went. Their huge empire was ruled by emperors and their first emperor was Augustus. He ruled quite well – but then, in AD 9, he made a b-i-g mistake.

Augustus put his nephew Varus in charge of the armies in Germany. BAD idea, Augustus.

✤ Varus thought he was a great warrior – he wasn't.

✤ Varus thought the local tribes loved him – they didn't.

✤ Varus thought the legions were unbeatable – they weren't.

A local chief, Herman (a German), led the Romans into a trap in Teutoburger Forest. When they got lost on the twisting paths, Herman's Germans turned and hacked them down. The legions, and the families who went with them, were cut to pieces. Roman guts were hung from the trees.

Varus fell on his sword and killed himself. The shame was too much. His head was sent to Uncle Emperor Augustus. And Augustus went mad for a while. He wandered around his palace for weeks. He kept banging his head against the walls and crying out:

✤ The German warriors wiped out three Roman legions, the 17th, the 18th and the 19th legions. Rome never again used those numbers for a legion. They thought they were unlucky.

✤ The Roman Empire stopped at the River Rhine. After this battle it never got any further north and the Germans stayed free of Roman rule.

✤ Herman the German became a German hero ever after.

But the REAL trouble with Teutoburger came later. The tribes said, 'Ooooh! See that? The Romans CAN be beaten after all. We'll try it again sometime.'

It wasn't the end of the Roman Empire. But it was the start of the end.

18 JULY AD 64

THE GREAT FIRE OF ROME

Sausages. The history of the world was maybe changed by a sausage. Amazing.

In Rome there was a great wooden arena called the Circus Maximus. On 18 July AD 64 there were chariot races going on inside. Outside there were people selling food to the hungry fans. To keep his sausages hot, the seller had a pan full of hot coals. You can guess what happened next…

The fire spread around the city and a huge area of Rome was destroyed.

When the fire was out the Roman people started to gossip. They said the crazy Emperor Nero had wanted houses cleared to make way for as new golden palace. This fire was probably Nero's trick to clear the houses! 'Nero played the fiddle as Rome burned,' they said. Nero was on holiday at the time of the fire, but when he got back he found the angry mob were blaming him for the fire.

> It wasn't me, honest. I've heard it was that bunch of Jews that call themselves Christians. Blame the Christians.

The innocent Christians were hunted down and massacred. The Roman writer, Tacitus, said:

> Nero turned the blame on the people called Christians. Vast numbers were found guilty and the spite of the Romans went with them to their deaths. They were covered with the skins of wild beasts and torn to death by dogs; or they were fastened on crosses; and, when it grew dark, they were burned to serve as lamps by night.

But Nero didn't manage to destroy all of the Christians. Instead they fought and became stronger. In the end they took over much of the world. And all because of a sausage spark.

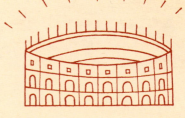

ROME, AD 80
OPENING THE COLOSSEUM

HAPPY HOLIDAY HAPPENINGS AT YOUR ALL-NEW COLOSSEUM – OPENS THIS WEEK!!!

❋

The colosseum opens at last and our noble emperor TITUS says
it's a public HOLIDAY!
So why not come along and join in the FUN?

❋

In the MORNING see … CHARIOTEERS do dangerous shunts and stunts,
enormous ELEPHANTS, with their trainers, doing tricks. Watch these elephants fight
against BEARS, LIONS and gladiators. Hunters have searched AFRICA to bring you
LEOPARDS, CHEETAHS, RHINOS AND CROCODILES. Gladiators will chase and
slay PIGS, BULLS, WILD BOAR, OSTRICHES and CAMELS.
WOMEN will be among the hunters!
Hear them CRY … then see them DIE!!!

❋

After every slaughter the wooden floor will be scattered with a fresh
COLOURED SAND.
Have a tasty LUNCH while you watch EXECUTIONS. See criminals and Christians
be TORN APART by wild animals, CRUCIFIED and BURNED ALIVE.

❋

In the AFTERNOON see … GLADIATORS fight to a certain death. And finally
watch a mock SEA BATTLE as the arena is FLOODED.
3,000 men fight till the water turns RED. In these opening games
9,000 animals will die and hundreds of humans. BE THERE and
DON'T DARE miss the fantastic FEAST OF FUN.

❋

May the gods bless Emperor Titus for our free entertainment.

The Romans didn't just kill their enemies in massacres and battles. They killed them for SPORT. The mighty Colosseum took eight years to build and could hold 50,000 people – big as a modern sports stadium. The Romans could watch gladiators, animal hunts and even sea battles. The opening of the Colosseum was to be the goriest games the world had ever seen.

After Emperor Trajan won great battles victories in Dacia in AD 107, he decided to have a party with Colosseum games killing 11,000 animals and 10,000 gladiators. Those games went on for 123 days. They ran out of animals to slaughter.

Over the next 300 years, half a million people and over a million wild animals died in the Colosseum 'games'. Ruthless Romans.

GERMANY, 31 DECEMBER AD 406
CROSSING THE RIVER RHINE

The Roman Empire was huge. The Roman army was powerful. So how did it end up beaten and broken? Lousy luck. And ice ... a cruel killer in a few history horrors, as you'll see.

The Romans pointed to the River Rhine map and said…

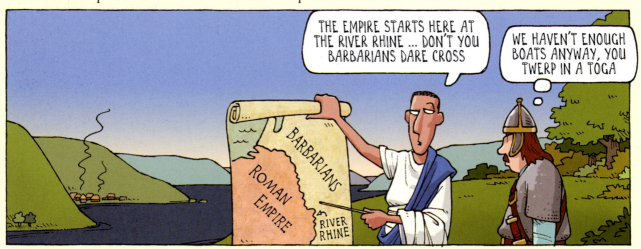

❀ But then, on 31 December AD 406, the River Rhine froze over. Tribes of barbarians – Vandals – were running away from their horrid Hun enemies. They escaped across the icy River Rhine.

❀ The Romans weren't expecting them. The Vandals started attacking and robbing Roman towns. It was all so easy they just kept going. They attacked Spain and North Africa before finally heading to Rome.

❀ By AD 410, the Goths had reached Rome too, and easily defeated the Romans. The mighty Roman Empire wouldn't last much longer. Beaten by Jack Frost.

The other problem was Rome's lousy leaders: the emperors. It's almost as if you HAD to be slightly potty to be a Roman ruler! Here are a few foul facts about the rotten Roman rulers. Only the odd word has been left out for you to complete…

1 Tiberius (AD 14-37) said that he would smash the _____ of anyone who disobeyed him.

2 Caligula (AD 37-41) wanted someone to help him to rule so he gave the job to his _____.

3 Claudius (AD 41-54) had his _____ executed.

4 Nero (AD 54-68) tried to drown his _____.

5 Augustus Caesar (31 BC-AD 14) caught Brutus, the murderer of Julius Caesar, and had his _____ thrown at the feet of Caesar's statue.

6 Elagabalus (AD 218-222) had the curious hobby of collecting every _____ he could find.

7 Honorius (AD 395-423) had a _____ called 'Rome'.

8 Vitellius (AD 69) had his _____ thrown in the River Tiber at Rome.

9 Hadrian (AD 117-138) forced a _____ to commit suicide.

10 Antonius (AD 138-161) died of eating too much _____.

MISSING WORDS

mother, head, chicken, horse, corpse, cobweb, cheese, wife, wrinkly, leg.

Answers

1 leg. Tiberius died at the age of 78, probably suffocated by his chief helper.

2 horse. Cruel Caligula liked to feed criminals to wild animals. He was stabbed to death by one of his guards.

3 wife. She was a bit of a flirt. But he also had 300 of her party friends chopped too!

4 mother. When the plot failed he sent soldiers to chop her. He stabbed himself to death before his enemies got to him.
His niece had him poisoned with mushrooms.

5 head. It didn't hurt.

6 cobweb. Maybe he was planning to build the world's first website?

7 chicken. Trouble is he loved the chicken Rome more than he loved the city Rome. He neglected the city.

8 corpse. He was murdered in the centre of Rome but not given a nice Emperor's burial.

9 wrinkly. Hadrian accused Servianus of treason and forced him to kill himself. But Servianus was 90 years old and hardly a big threat.

10 cheese. At least that's what a Roman historian blamed. Guess it was just hard cheese.

THE FIRST VIKING RAID

The Vikings from Denmark and Norway were the most menacing men of the deadly Dark Ages. They conquered parts of Russia, Britain, Ireland and France ... but where did it all begin?

The monks at Lindisfarne lived a quiet life. A bit of fishing, growing vegetables and a lot of praying. They were in for a shock…

The Vikings landed and started robbing the monastery. The monks couldn't fight and they didn't have weapons. The Vikings had an easy time.

Some monks were slaughtered, some were driven into the sea to drown, some were taken away to be slaves.

The Vikings became the greatest slave traders in the world at that time.

The Vikings enjoyed their chopping trip so much they came back again and again until in the end they settled in England and took over the whole of the north. English King Alfred the Great saved the south of England.

BUT … although the Vikings were good at fighting helpless monks, they were not so tough when it came to fighting people who fought back. A year after their Lindisfarne raid they attacked a monastery on the River Tyne to the south.

This time the people of the towns on the Tyne were ready for them. The Viking leader was captured. The Tyneside people sent him back to the Viking longships… in a box. He'd been chopped into pieces.

❧ DID YOU KNOW? ❧

The monks of England kept a diary of events, the Anglo-Saxon Chronicle. In 793, it says there were signs of doom in the weather…

In this year fierce, dark omens came over the land of Northumbria. There were terrible whirlwinds, lightning storms, and fiery dragons were seen flying in the sky. These signs were followed by great famine.

The storms and dragons were a sign that God was annoyed, some people said. Alcuin, an English monk wrote:

Never before has such terror appeared in Britain as we have now suffered. The heathens poured out the blood of saints around the altar, and trampled on the bodies of saints in the temple of God, like dung in the streets.

Trampled bodies of saints like poo? Vicious Vikings.

ENGLAND, NOVEMBER AD 869
KILLING OF KING EDMUND

King Edmund was a saintly Christian ruler in East Anglia, England. But he came up against the Vikings ... who were not very saintly when it came to executing their enemies...

HI THERE. TODAY WE'RE GOING TO SHOW YOU HOW TO KILL A STUBBORN CHRISTIAN KING ... TO HELP ME I HAVE KING EDMUND OF ANGLIA

HI THERE

FIRST YOU TIE YOUR VICTIM TO A TREE

NOW GET YOUR FRIENDS ALONG TO FILL HIM FULL OF ARROWS

IT'S AN OAK, NOT A JOKE, FOLK

NOW TURN HIM AROUND TO FACE THE TREE AND START TO SNAP HIS RIBS OFF HIS SPINE. SPREAD THE RIBS LIKE BRANCHES OF A TREE...

S-PINE TREE ... PINE TREE ... GEDDIT?

PULL OUT HIS LUNGS AND SPREAD THEM OVER HIS BACK LIKE THE WINGS OF AN EAGLE

AND FINISH OFF BY LOPPING OFF THE HEAD

DON'T TRY THIS AT HOME

Some historians say it never happened – Edmund died in battle and the Vikings made up stories about the Blood Eagle torture to scare their enemies.

There are other stories about Edmund's death. One says his head was thrown into a wood and a wolf guarded it. Even though the wolf was hungry it didn't eat the head. It stayed with the head till Edmund's people found it and took it off to be buried with the body.

How did they find Ed's head? It cried out, 'Herc, here, here!'

The English built a church for the two bits of Edmund. When it was finished they dug up the corpse to put it in the new church. The arrow wounds had healed and the head was joined back on the body. 'A miracle of God,' the people cried. (There was a red line round the neck where it had been cut off. God wasn't a very good doctor.)

AD 1000
VIKINGS LAND IN AMERICA

The Vicious Vikings had l-o-n-g, dark winters so they made up stories to pass the time. Some of these stories were made up Fiking fibs ... or Viking vibs.

It's said that in AD 986 a Viking called Bjarni set off to sail from Norway to Greenland … but missed. He hit America by mistake.

YA, IT WAS SOME TRIP, WE GOT LOST, WE DISCOVERED AMERICA AND WE GOT WORMS

On his way back he sailed into a patch of ship-worms who nibbled his wooden boat till it sank. Luckily his spare boat was worm-proof.

The Viking explorer, Leif Ericsson, heard Bjarni's story and went across to America to have a look. Then Leif's brother, Thorvald, went across to stay. Thorvald's Vikings met the Native Americans who screamed at them … so the Vikings called the natives 'skraelings' because that means 'screamers'.

The Vikings were not sure if the skraelings were friendly. What do you do if you are not sure?

WE DO NOT WANT TO HARM YOU

YES ... WELL, WE'LL KILL YOU, JUST TO BE ON THE SAFE SIDE

After the killing the rest of the natives ran off. They came back with a large force. Thorvald was shot in the stomach with an arrow. It was fired by a man with one leg … maybe he once had a wooden leg but it was eaten by woodworm?

MAYBE IF WE SCREAM AT THEM THEY'LL GO AWAY

THE VIKINGS HAD A PROBLEM...

DO WE CARRY HIM BACK TO THE BOAT AND SAVE HIM?

IF WE CARRY THORVALD WE CAN'T FIGHT. WE COULD ALL DIE!

SO DO WE DIG A QUICK GRAVE AND BURY HIM HERE?

EXCUSE ME LADS, BUT I'M NOT DEAD YET!

GOOD POINT

WE NEED TO KNOW IF HE'LL LIVE OR DIE

HOW DO WE DO THAT?

EASY! A WISE OLD DOCTOR TAUGHT ME THIS TRICK...

FIRST YOU COOK SOME PORRIDGE AND STIR IN SOME ONIONS...

SCRUMMY!

NOW YOU FEED IT TO ME...

OPEN WIDE FOR MUMMY

NOW SNIFF MY BELLY. IF THE ARROW HAS GONE CLEAN THROUGH YOU'LL SMELL THE ONIONS. I'M AS GOOD AS DEAD...

I SMELL ONIONS!

BURY HIM!

YES ... NO ... WAIT ... THAT WISE OLD DOCTOR WAS PRETTY STUPID, NOW I COME TO THINK OF IT...

THORVALD DIED AND THE VIKINGS BURIED HIM.

THE NORMAN CONQUEST

Some Vikings moved south into France. The French king gave them a northern bit of his country just to keep them happy. These 'North-men' became the 'Normans'. One really fierce Norman, Duke William, started looking around for more land to conquer. He picked on England. In 1066, he landed on the south coast and met the English King Harold in battle at Hastings. He won.

It's England's most famous battle but how much do you know about it? Just answer True or False…

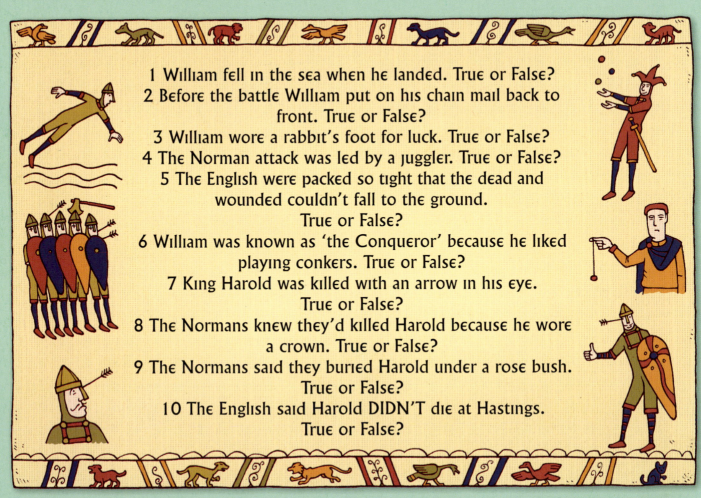

1 William fell in the sea when he landed. True or False?

2 Before the battle William put on his chain mail back to front. True or False?

3 William wore a rabbit's foot for luck. True or False?

4 The Norman attack was led by a juggler. True or False?

5 The English were packed so tight that the dead and wounded couldn't fall to the ground. True or False?

6 William was known as 'the Conqueror' because he liked playing conkers. True or False?

7 King Harold was killed with an arrow in his eye. True or False?

8 The Normans knew they'd killed Harold because he wore a crown. True or False?

9 The Normans said they buried Harold under a rose bush. True or False?

10 The English said Harold DIDN'T die at Hastings. True or False?

Answers

1 True. He stumbled and fell forward as he reached the beach. Ooops! His men gasped. A bad sign. But witty Will grabbed some pebbles, stood up and said, 'See how I have grabbed England?'

2 True. It was another unlucky sign. William just laughed and said, 'This is the day I "turn" from Duke to King.'

3 False. William wore the bones of Saint Rasyphus and Saint Ravennus around his neck for luck.

4 True. The Normans didn't want to attack up hill and risk their lives. At 9 a.m. the minstrel Taillefer began to juggle with his sword and sing a battle song. He attacked – an English warrior moved forward to meet him and Taillefer lopped off his head. Taillefer moved on – the English shields parted to let him through where they hacked him down. He died.

5 True.

6 False.

7 False. Harold was WOUNDED with an arrow to the eye. But he was KILLED when Norman knights charged forward and hacked him to bits.

8 False. Harold's face was smashed. Only his wife knew his corpse because she could spot its secret marks.

9 False. They said King Harold's corpse was taken to the sea shore and buried under a pile of stones. The English gave him a headstone reading, 'Harold, you rest here, to guard the sea and shore.'

10 True. The English told a story that Harold survived, buried under a pile of bodies. A peasant woman found him and nursed him back to health. He hid in a cellar in Winchester for two years before leading attacks on the hated Normans. In time he got religion and became Harold the hermit.

THE CHILDREN'S CRUSADE

The Normans took over from the Vikings as the bullies of Europe. The posh Normans trained as knights, and then set off looking for someone to kill. In 1095, the pope gave them an excuse. Pope Urban II told the knights of Europe NOT to kill other Christian knights. But they COULD kill Muslims in the Holy Land.

THE TURKS CUT OPEN THE BELLIES OF CHRISTIANS THAT THEY WANT TO TORMENT WITH A LOATHSOME DEATH. THEY TEAR OUT THEIR ORGANS AND TIE THEM TO A STAKE. THEY DRAG THEIR VICTIMS ROUND THE STAKE AND FLOG THEM. THEY KILL THEM AS THEY LIE FLAT ON THE GROUND WITH THEIR GUTS OUT.

AND THAT'S NOT ALL ... THEY TIE CHRISTIANS TO POSTS AND SHOOT THEM FULL OF ARROWS. THEY ORDER OTHERS TO BARE THEIR NECKS AND ATTACK THEM WITH SWORDS TRYING TO SEE IF THEY CAN CUT OFF THEIR HEADS WITH A SINGLE STROKE.

The Christians of Europe went to the Holy Land to capture holy sites, like Jerusalem. The Muslims who lived there put up a fight and so wars started. They were known as the Crusades. They were a waste of lives, but the craziest crusade of all was the Children's Crusade where children tried to join in the Crusading fun.

Once upon a time there was a little shepherd boy called Stephen of Cloyes. One morning he woke up and said, 'I have seen Jesus.'

'Ooooh!' his friends cried. 'You are more holy than your socks!'

Stephen said, 'Jesus wants us children to capture the Holy Land for his church. I am marching off next month. Follow me. God will look after us because we are children.'

The children grew very excited and cried out things like, 'I'm excited,' and 'My mum wants to ground me but I'm going anyway,' and, 'Where's the Holy Land? We didn't do that in Geography.'

Anyway, 30,000 French children came together – mostly boys around 12 years old, but some gutsy girls too. They marched through the towns and villages, carrying banners, candles, and crosses and singing. It was such a happy sound. 'Tra-la!'

Thousands of French children climbed onto ships. They asked the sailors, 'Dear friends, are you sailing us to the Holy Land?'

And the sailors replied, 'Don't be silly, children. We are sailing you off to Egypt to be sold as slaves!' And those children weren't singing tra-la any more. Instead they were saying, 'Oh bother. I thought God was supposed to look after us.'

And no one lived happy ever after ... except the slave traders, of course.

The End

Some say the story of Stephen is a lie ... a myth. The truth is the 'Children's' Crusade was more a crusade of the poor peasants — old and young, men and women. The Children's Crusade would NOT look like a school trip. More like a mob of unpleasant peasants.

Caffa City, 1347
BLACK DEATH STRIKES

Sometimes you can kill your enemies by giving them a disease. The trouble is you can end up causing the biggest disaster the world has ever seen. The Black Death began in the Middle East and ended up killing half the people in Europe. There is a horrible historical story that says it wasn't bad luck ... it was germ warfare.

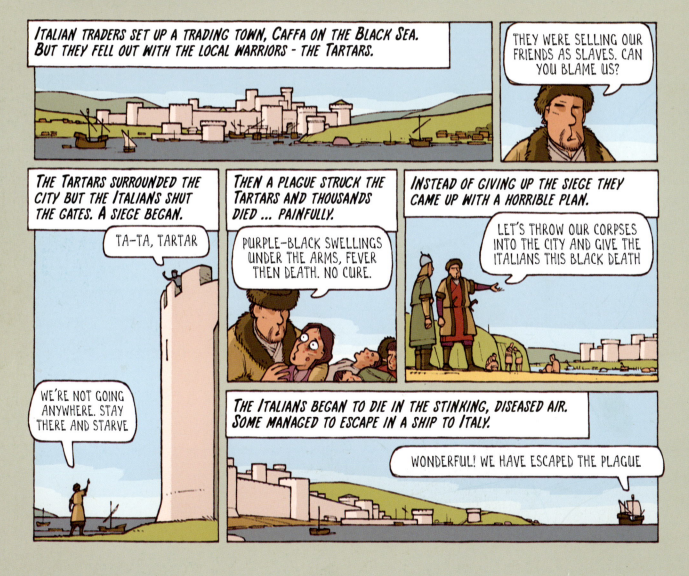

ITALIAN TRADERS SET UP A TRADING TOWN, CAFFA ON THE BLACK SEA. BUT THEY FELL OUT WITH THE LOCAL WARRIORS - THE TARTARS.

THEY WERE SELLING OUR FRIENDS AS SLAVES. CAN YOU BLAME US?

THE TARTARS SURROUNDED THE CITY BUT THE ITALIANS SHUT THE GATES. A SIEGE BEGAN.

TA-TA, TARTAR

WE'RE NOT GOING ANYWHERE. STAY THERE AND STARVE

THEN A PLAGUE STRUCK THE TARTARS AND THOUSANDS DIED ... PAINFULLY.

PURPLE-BLACK SWELLINGS UNDER THE ARMS, FEVER THEN DEATH. NO CURE.

INSTEAD OF GIVING UP THE SIEGE THEY CAME UP WITH A HORRIBLE PLAN.

LET'S THROW OUR CORPSES INTO THE CITY AND GIVE THE ITALIANS THIS BLACK DEATH

THE ITALIANS BEGAN TO DIE IN THE STINKING, DISEASED AIR. SOME MANAGED TO ESCAPE IN A SHIP TO ITALY.

WONDERFUL! WE HAVE ESCAPED THE PLAGUE

Of course they hadn't escaped. The plague was carried by fleas that lived on black rats. Once the plague rat had died the fleas could jump onto the nearest human and pass it on.

The story says the Caffa sailors carried the plague with them back to Italy and from there it spread across Europe. The truth is it would have reached Europe sooner or later anyway.

Northern France, 26 August 1346
BATTLE OF CRÉCY

The Middle Ages. Knights in shining armour riding horses into battle. No one can beat them, can they? Oh yes they can. Soldiers are always looking for better ways to kill their enemies. The English armies found ways of using the longbow and arrows to smash the French.

The English king, Edward III, said HE should be king of France so he sailed across with about 10,000 men. French king Philip VI had at least twice as many — maybe five times as many men. And the French had lots of knights. The English had lots of peasants with longbows.

Oh dear, looked like English head Ed would soon be dead Ed.

What happened next? Imagine a Welsh archer with Ed's army. What would he have written to his wife?

Dear Megan

What a day. The good news is I am still alive. How? I do not know. There were ten Frenchies for every Welsh and English man, I tell you. Cor! Our King Edward made camp at the top of a hill near Crécy village. He looked out from the top of a windmill. 'Right lads,' he said, 'they'll attack tomorrow morning, but we'll dig traps with sharp stakes to stop their charging horses.'

When he said 'we'll dig', he meant us archers would do the digging. Hard work, love. No sooner had we started than those Frenchies were on the move. They couldn't wait till morning to attack. Their knights were desperate to fight before night. King Philip couldn't stop them. The evening sun was in their eyes, and they didn't really have a plan.

Well, they had a sort of plan. They ordered their men with crossbows to shoot down our front rows. But the crossbow men weren't ready. They'd left their shields in the supply wagons. Then there was a shower of rain and it wet the crossbow strings didn't it? We rolled up our longbow strings and kept them dry. Then it was our longbows against their dripping crossbows. It was murder.

We were firing twelve shots a minute … the French crossbows could only manage two. They fell like geese at Christmas. The living started to turn and run back. But the French knights were riding forward by then. They trampled all over their own bowmen. Hah! Laugh? We were wetting ourselves.

The French knights rode on towards us but they had to cross a swampy stream. Our arrows punched holes in their armour and bigger holes in their horses.

Of course a few French knights got through and even reached Edward's son, the Black Prince. Fine lad. He sent a message to the king saying, 'I could do with a bit of help, Dad,' but the king sent back to say, 'Look after yourself, son.' Even tougher than my dad if you ask me.

Anyway, the French were driven back and King Philip told them to retreat. They left a lot of wounded French knights on the ground and stuck in the mud. Our lads ran down to the wounded French knights. One of them said to me, 'I surrender … my family will pay a ransom.'

I just said, 'Sorry, boyo … I'm a Welsh peasant. We do things different in Wales.' And I took my best knife and I pushed it into the joints in the armour. Just where the helmet joins the neck piece. Cccct!

The king gave us something better than a ransom – he gave us each an acre of land to farm when we get home. If you ask me this war won't last a hundred days, love. So I'll see you soon.

Love to my mum and the kids.

Ianto.

The Battle of Crécy was just the start of the terrible, long war. Kings came and went. It didn't last a 100 days … it lasted over 100 years. It was called The Hundred Years War.

And the power of the longbow meant it would soon mean the end for the knight in armour.

France, 14th May 1431
DEATH OF JOAN OF ARC

The Hundred Years War went on through years of plague, peasant revolts and lots of dead kings. Who would win in the end? A great warrior like Edward III with his longbow power? No. The French with a great warrior who had petticoat power – Joan of Arc.

Joan was a shepherd girl. She said an angel had told her to lead the French into battle against the English. She did and she won. Of course the English were furious. Beaten. By a girl?

Then they captured her. But you can't execute an enemy leader. It isn't sporting. They had to come up with a sneaky reason. The Bible told them…

A woman is a witch, a snake, a plague, a rat, a rash, a poison, a burning flame and an assistant of the Devil.

They can't execute an enemy leader … but they CAN execute a witch. Joan was put on trial.

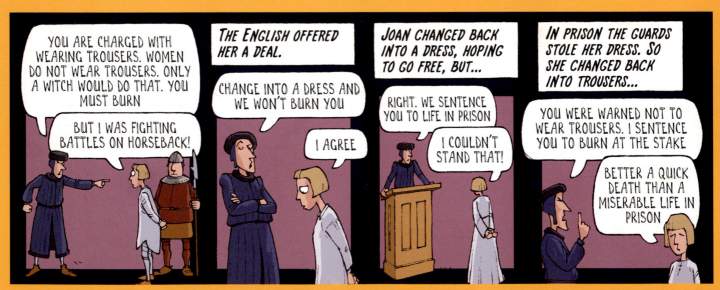

YOU ARE CHARGED WITH WEARING TROUSERS. WOMEN DO NOT WEAR TROUSERS. ONLY A WITCH WOULD DO THAT. YOU MUST BURN

BUT I WAS FIGHTING BATTLES ON HORSEBACK!

THE ENGLISH OFFERED HER A DEAL.

CHANGE INTO A DRESS AND WE WON'T BURN YOU

I AGREE

JOAN CHANGED BACK INTO A DRESS, HOPING TO GO FREE, BUT...

RIGHT. WE SENTENCE YOU TO LIFE IN PRISON

I COULDN'T STAND THAT!

IN PRISON THE GUARDS STOLE HER DRESS. SO SHE CHANGED BACK INTO TROUSERS...

YOU WERE WARNED NOT TO WEAR TROUSERS. I SENTENCE YOU TO BURN AT THE STAKE

BETTER A QUICK DEATH THAN A MISERABLE LIFE IN PRISON

So Joan of Arc was burned to death – NOT as an enemy but as a 'witch'. The English burned her body three times till there was nothing but ash. That was scattered in the river.

It did the evil English no good. In the end they lost the war. Joan became a French saint.

ENGLAND, 29 MARCH 1461
BATTLE OF TOWTON

Slaughter often happened AFTER a battle in the Middle Ages, when one side was trying to escape. The winners chased after the losers and finished them off. Sometimes the armies agreed that the winner would show mercy – but sometimes they AGREED that winners could slaughter the losers. That's what happened at the Battle of Towton in England…

The war was between the York family of England (whose badge was a white rose), and the Lancaster family of England (whose badge was a red rose). The battles were known as the 'Wars of the Roses'.

But the Battle of Towton was the bloodiest battle of that war – probably the bloodiest ever seen in Britain.

If there had been newspapers in 1461 it might have looked like this…

The Towton Times

30 March 1461

HOW TO LOOK GOOD DEAD

MIDDLE AGES SPREAD? TRY OUR NEW PEASANT DIET – GET A LOCAL ARMY TO STEAL YOUR FOOD

TERROR AT TOWTON

What a battle! I write to you from a cold Yorkshire moor, in a field they are calling 'Bloody Meadow'.

King Edward led the White Roses into the battle and told them, 'No quarter!' so it was NO prisoners. Winner kills all. The Reds stood ready for battle on the morning of Palm Sunday 29 March. A huge army with one thing missing … luck. As the Whites faced them, a fierce snow storm blew across the moor, straight into the faces of the Reds.

White arrows sailed from the sky. The Reds tried to fire back but the wind meant the red arrows fell short.

The Red commander shouted, 'Charge!' He had to really. They couldn't just sit there under our arrow storm. As our readers know, the side that charges first usually loses the battle. The Whites stood ready to meet them, hand to hand.

Soon the fighting had stopped. You'll never guess why? The bodies were piled so high, we – the live fighters – couldn't get to each other. They had to clear the battlefield first.

CUT THEIR THROATS

Of course not all the bodies were dead … many were just wounded. We had to finish them off. Cut their throats.

When the Whites' Duke of Norfolk arrived to help us with fresh men, the Red Roses cracked, and tried to run away over a stream called Cock beck. The Whites caught them

knee deep in water. The Whites chased the Reds over Cock beck and didn't even get their feet wet. They were walking over dead bodies.

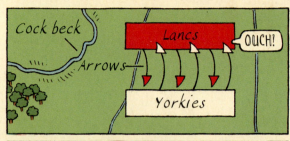

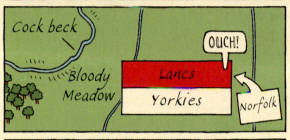

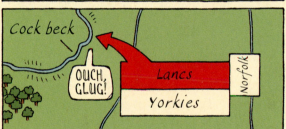

SO MANY DEAD REDS

Bridges across the streams collapsed with all those Red Rose running men over them, and a lot drowned.

The killing went on all night.

It's morning now. With so many dead Reds it has to be the end of these Wars of the Roses.

Of course it wasn't. The wars really ended 20 years later when White Yorkist Richard III lost to Red Lancastrian Henry Tudor. The plaguey Middle Ages made way for the dreadful days of the terrible Tudors.

41

3 AUGUST 1492
CHRISTOPHER COLUMBUS SETS OFF FOR AMERICA

In the 1400s explorers began to travel further and further around the world to seek gold and silver, spices and slaves. On 3 August 1492 Christopher Columbus (an Italian working for Spain) set off to find a way to China, in the East, by travelling West. Instead he bumped into America.

Chris and his Spanish masters wanted gold, land, gold, slaves and gold. The land and the gold belonged to the Indians*, of course, but that didn't matter to the savage Spanish. CC met Indians and wrote…

At daybreak a great number of men came to the shore. I listened very carefully to them and tried to find out if they had any gold. I gathered from their signs that if I sailed south I would find a king with great cups full of gold. I could conquer all of these people with just fifty men and rule them as I please!

✿ Before CC set off back to Spain he kidnapped around 20 Indians. The terrible conditions on the ships meant only around seven arrived in Spain alive. They were enough to show the Spanish that these strong Indians would make great slaves. CC headed back to America – and this time he had 1,200 soldiers armed with guns, swords, cannon and attack dogs.

✿ CC's slaves had to grow food for his army, dig for gold or spin cotton. The Indians weren't allowed to say, 'No'. Indians who disobeyed would have their noses cut off or their ears lopped. They'd be sent back to the village as a warning to the others.

NO NO, OR NO NOSE

* CC always believed he had landed in Asia (or 'the Indies' as it was known) and that's why he called the natives 'Indians'.

✿ In 1495, the Spanish rounded up 500 Arawak Indians on Haiti to be sent back to Spain, and took another 500 to work for them on other islands. Half the slaves died on the journey, but CC shrugged and said…

> *Although they die now they will not always die. We can send all the slaves from here that you can sell!*

But he was wrong. Forced work and dreadful diseases killed all the Arawaks off in time.

✿ By 1516, the Spanish were having to bring in slaves from other American Indian lands. They were packed into ships like sardines on supermarket shelves. They were locked in to stop them escaping and they died in the filthy, scorching air. Spanish history writer, Peter Martyr, said…

> *You didn't need a compass to find your way along the slave ship routes… All you had to do was follow the trail of dead Indians that had to be thrown overboard.*

When the Spaniards ran out of Indian slaves the Spanish in America started buying them in Africa and taking them across the Atlantic to work there. CC began the terrible slave trade that lasted another 400 years.

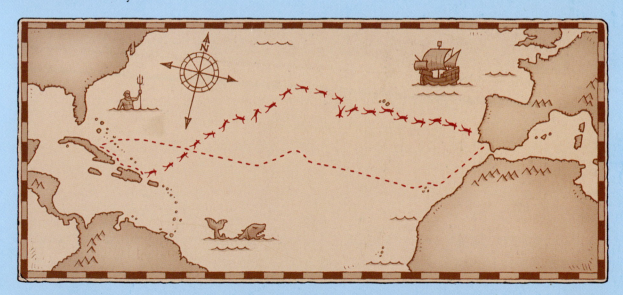

LUTHER AND THE CHURCH DOOR

A man nailed a bit of paper to a church door. Millions have died since that simple but awful act.

The trouble was that most people in Europe believed what the church told them. Priests said, 'Give us your cash and we will have a word with God. He'll make sure you go to heaven. So pay up.' The payments were called 'indulgences'. Then the Pope decided to build an even bigger palace for himself in Rome. He needed money, so he ordered his priests, 'Charge more for the indulgences!'

A German monk, Martin Luther, was angry. He said the Pope was rich enough ... and, anyway, indulgences were a daft idea. God would let people into heaven without them. Luther wrote his ideas on this paper and nailed them to the church door at All Saints Church in Wittenberg.

Lots of people agreed with Luther and made their own church – the Protestant Church. And THAT made endless trouble ... since Luther's time millions of Protestants have been horribly slaughtered by Catholics – millions of Catholics have been horribly slaughtered by Protestants. Some of the world's worst horrible history has been Christians hating Christians. They have...

...roasted children over an open fire and peeled off the skin of living men.

...chopped off hands and feet and thrown them over town walls.

...thrown women down wells and piled stones on top of them.

...pulled out the eyes of soldiers and sliced off their noses and lips.

...tortured priests by stretching them on racks till their bones cracked.

...nipped off lumps of flesh with red-hot pincers.

...hanged men in their own gardens while their wives and children watched.

...beheaded an old lady with 20 axe blows.

...hanged people in chains and left them to die slowly.

So, Martin Luther nailed his list to the church door at Wittenberg. That's what teacher will tell you. But DID he? That story was told in 1546, almost 30 years after it happened. The story says Luther decorated the door on 31 October 1517. But he didn't go to Wittenberg till 1518. The truth? He SENT his proclamation to his bishop and archbishop. Mailed not nailed.

20 SEPTEMBER 1519
FERDINAND MAGELLAN SAILS THE WORLD

Rich people in Europe wanted silks, gems and spices from China and Japan. Could they get these riches quicker by sailing around the south tip of South America?

Ferdinand Magellan was a Portuguese sailor who went to work for the Spanish. He hoped to find a way to sail around South America. He left Spain on 20 September 1519 with five ships and about 237 men. At first he did not tell his men where they were going because he thought they would be too scared to obey him.

Magellan found a way round the southern tip of South America and set off west again. But Magellan and his men suffered terrible hunger and disease. They ran out of fresh food and many died of scurvy.

We ate only old biscuit that had turned to powder, and full of grubs, and stinking from the dirt which the rats had made on it when eating the good biscuit. We drank water that was yellow and reeking. The men were so hungry that if any of them caught a rat, he could sell it for a high price to someone who would eat it.

Only 18 of the 237 men made it back to Spain. But Magellan wasn't one of them. He didn't starve. He died even more horribly…

❧ Magellan and his crew landed on Cebu Island in the Philippines.
❧ There was a war going on between two tribes on Cebu and Mactan.
❧ Magellan and his sailors agreed to help the king attack the island of Mactan. Bad idea.
❧ Magellan took a poisoned Cebu arrow in the foot and a spear through the heart.
❧ He died on 27 April 1521 and his body was left behind.

So Magellan, famous for being the first man to sail around the world … didn't.

Not even his corpse made it all the way.

DESTRUCTION OF THE AZTECS

The explorers from Europe met many native people in the Americas. The Aztecs of Mexico were not very pleasant people.

✸ They attacked other tribes and sacrificed their prisoners to the gods.

✸ The victims were taken to the top of a pyramid and had their beating hearts ripped out with stone knives.

✸ The corpses were thrown down the side of the blood-soaked pyramid.

✸ In one festival they killed 20,000 victims.

Then a little Spanish army arrived in Mexico, led by Hernando Cortes…

The Aztec warriors danced for the Spanish visitors. But the Spanish thought the Aztecs planned to kill them after the dance … even though the dancers had no weapons.

The Spanish struck first. A report said:

The Spanish ran in among the dancers and attacked the man who was drumming and cut off his arms. They cut off his head and it rolled across the floor.

Then they attacked the dancers, stabbing them, spearing them and striking some with their swords. They also killed the Aztecs in the audience.

They attacked some from behind and these fell instantly to the ground with their guts hanging out. Some Aztec dancers tried to run away but their intestines dragged as they ran; they seemed to tangle their feet in their own entrails.

Others were beheaded; the Spanish cut off their heads or split their heads to pieces. They struck others in the shoulders, and their arms were torn from their bodies. No matter how they tried to save themselves, the Aztecs could find no escape.

Some Aztecs tried to force their way out, but the Spaniards murdered them at the gates. Others climbed the walls, but they could not save themselves. Those who lay down among the victims and pretended to be dead were safe for a while. But if they stood up again, the Spaniards saw them and killed them.

The blood of the warriors flowed like water and gathered into pools. The pools widened, and the stench of blood and guts filled the air.

✿ The slaughter was the start of a war. There were very few Spanish soldiers in Mexico but they fought with crossbows, guns, cannon, armour, attack dogs, horses and even hunting birds.
✿ The Aztecs had wooden clubs and stone knives.
✿ The Spanish defeated the Aztecs. Weapon power wins again.
Should we feel sorry for the heart-ripping Aztecs? Probably not. The Aztecs were heartless … but not as heartless as their prisoners.

I'VE GOT A BAD FEELING ABOUT THIS

ST BARTHOLOMEW'S DAY MASSACRE

In 1572, Princess Margaret of France, a Catholic, married King Henry of Navarre, a Protestant. But Margaret's mother, Catherine, hated Protestants – and she had a plan to get rid of them. She invited all the Protestant lords to the wedding in Paris. They could all be killed together! Clever, eh? The people of Paris would help ... they were furious because their princess was marrying a Protestant prince.

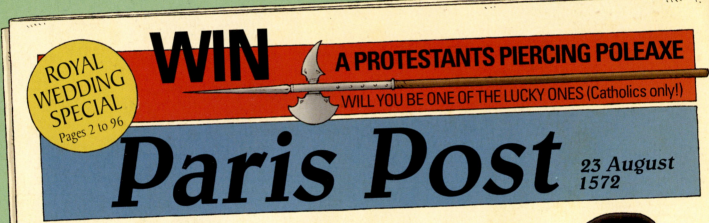

ROYAL WEDDING SPECIAL
Pages 2 to 96

WIN A PROTESTANTS PIERCING POLEAXE
WILL YOU BE ONE OF THE LUCKY ONES (Catholics only!)

Paris Post 23 August 1572

KILLING ON BART JUST THE START?

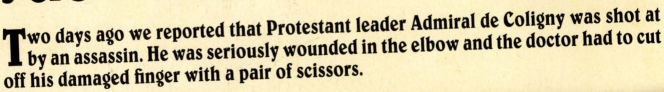

Two days ago we reported that Protestant leader Admiral de Coligny was shot at by an assassin. He was seriously wounded in the elbow and the doctor had to cut off his damaged finger with a pair of scissors.

Stabbed

The king's Catholic mother, Catherine, said, 'Nothing to do with me!' But the Paris people are armed and marched round to Coligny's house. The sick man was stabbed in the belly till his guts spilled out. He was still alive when they threw the man and his guts out of the window. He died. Luckily no one was walking under the window at the time.

DE COLIGNY (AND GUTS)

Paris mob rampage

Killing Coligny was like a starting pistol for a massacre of Protestants. The Paris mob rampaged through the streets. Chains were used to block streets so Protestants couldn't escape. Protestant women and children were hacked to pieces in cold blood. Dead Protestant bodies were thrown into the River Seine. Catholics held parties and processions to celebrate. What a way to celebrate St Bartholomew's day! As you know, Bart was the saint who was skinned alive, then beheaded.

They're in-Seine!

🦋 Some say 30,000 Protestants died in the massacres as the Paris attacks spread all round France. They had a chant like a football song … 'Kill, kill, kill them all!'

🦋 The Catholics also robbed their victims. One Protestant woman had her hands cut off so they could pinch her bracelets.

🦋 Of course there were revenge attacks by Protestants on Catholics that went on for years. Men and women were killed and their babies were 'christened' with their blood.

🦋 The Paris massacre was led Catholic Lord Guise … and he died in 1588. He was stabbed by 43 assassins' knives … he must have looked like a hedgehog. A very RED hedgehog.

This was not the last time Christians would massacre other Christians.

BUT OF COURSE WE HAVE THE POINTY BITS ON THE OUTSIDE

49

ENGLISH CHANNEL, 19 JULY 1588
SPANISH ARMADA

England became Protestant when King Henry VIII switched from being a Catholic. The Spanish wanted to invade and make the country Catholic again. A massive Spanish fleet should have smashed a fleet of 55 English ships. Why did the Spanish fail? Lousy luck...

AH ... ONE OF MY FAVOURITE PHRASES

I ❤ LOUSY LUCK

Queen Elizabeth I of England was waiting with her army and navy. She is famous for her speech to the troops as they waited for the Spanish to land …

I have the body of a weak and feeble woman, but I have the heart and stomach of a king.

Some historians are not sure if she made the speech. As for her 'heart', a lot of her soldiers said she had none. One soldier was punished for saying, 'When the Armada arrived Elizabeth was wetting herself with fear!'

MAYBE SHE JUST NEEDED THE LOO

The Spanish fleet waited off the coast of France for their soldiers to climb aboard. The English set fire to four old ships full of tar and gunpowder and sent them drifting into the Spanish fleet.

The fire-ships did little damage but the panicking Spanish cut their anchors, put up their sails and ran.

EEK

✹ A gale blew Spanish ships towards sandbanks and the shore. Many were grounded and trapped – sitting ducks for the English cannon. The next day the Spanish fleet fled to the North Sea, round the north of Scotland and west of Ireland.

✹ They were hit by even stronger gales … and they had no anchors to save them. (Those had been cut off). Twenty-four great galleons were wrecked and sailors washed ashore onto the west coast of Ireland. Only half of their ships made it home to Spain. The sailors were starving, short of fresh water and weak with disease.

LOUSY LUCK 2...

Philip had picked one of the stormiest years EVER. Far more Spanish ships and men were lost in the cold and the gales than in the battles. And that's lousy luck. As Philip said…

I sent my Armada to fight men. Instead they fought God's waves and winds.

Even the English said it was the wind what won it. Sailors were given a medal that said…

HE BLEW WITH HIS WINDS AND THEY WERE SCATTERED

HMM

Spanish survivors were shipwrecked in Ireland. Elizabeth ruled Ireland at that time and she said her soldiers could torture Spanish sailors if they caught them. Thousands of Spanish sailors swam ashore … and were captured and executed. Some were hanged and some beheaded.

Six young Dutch boys had been on board one ship. They were hanged

The ordinary Irish peasants didn't like the English. Many Irish helped the Spanish sailors washed ashore. But other stories said the Irish massacred Spanish sailors. One Irish soldier killed 80 Spaniards on the beach with his axe. The pain in Spain was awful.

THAT'S MY BOY

51

NORTH AMERICA, MAY 1607
VIRGINIA SETTLERS LAND

Some British settlers set off for America to find gold and landed in May 1607. They didn't seem to bother that they first had to find food. Gold before guts. They landed in Virginia and dug for gold in Jamestown instead of digging to plant crops.

Of course they began to starve. In the winter of 1609 came the 'Starving Time'. English settler, George Percy, wrote of their sufferings.

> We were driven, through hunger, to eat things it is not natural to eat. We ate the flesh and the excrement of man. As well as our own people we ate an Indian after he had been buried for three days. We ate him all.

FEET AND TWO VEG...

Imagine eating 'excrement' … that's poo.

...AND LOTS OF ROAST POTATOES

After that, some of the other tasty treats they ate must have seemed gorgeous! They ate…

dogs

rats

mice

snakes

horses

One man killed his wife and began to eat her! He had covered her in salt (so she'd get him through the winter). He was caught and hanged … but not eaten.

JUSTICE IS SERVED!

BUT NO DINNER

To add to their misery the Jamestown settlers fell ill. They suffered diseases like dysentery where they had bloody poo and one man died after…

The problem is that the water they were drinking was unhealthy stuff. George Percy said…

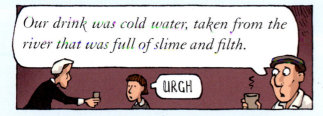

It could be that they were drinking the water too close to the spot where their toilets drained into.

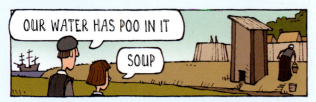

Life was tough for those early Virginia settlers – or 'Planters' as they called themselves. Between 1606 and 1625 there were 7,289 Planters landed and 6,040 of them were 'planted' in the ground, dead. Starvation, disease and Indian attacks killed them off. Planter Richard Frethorne wrote…

I didn't know a head could hold as much water as that which flows from my eyes every day.

He was dead within a year of writing that.

The Planters began to poison the Native American Indians so they could take more of their land. They offered the Indians a special Planters' beer … but the Planters didn't drink it. The Indian chief, his family and two hundred of his tribe dropped dead from poison.

But the Indians could be guilty of cruelty and treachery too. Chief Opechancanough sent a 'peace' party to talk to talk to the Planters. They ate breakfast together, then the Indians grabbed whatever weapons they could find and slaughtered every man, woman and child they could catch. They killed 350 Planters when there were only about 1,000 in the whole of Virginia.

Twenty-two years later Chief Opechancanough massacred over 300 of them again. But the Native American Indians would lose in the end. Horribly.

21 December 1620

PILGRIM FATHERS REACH AMERICA

In 1620, a group of English religious runaways, the Pilgrims, were offered land in Virginia, North America, in return for working there. They were supposed to start a new life. It led to quite a bit of death.

The Pilgrims left Plymouth, England, in their ship *Mayflower*. After a terrible trip of 102 days they landed in a storm. Oddly, the storm had driven them to land in a place in North America other sailors called 'Plymouth' … nowhere near Virginia, where they planned to be.

✤ The Pilgrims had no right to be there but they stayed anyway.

Oh…this'll do

✤ They hadn't thought about this settling lark. Pilgrim William Mullins took 126 pairs of shoes and 13 pairs of boots but NO ONE took a plough, a horse, a cow or even a fishing line.

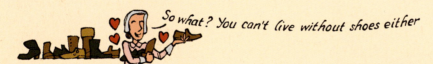

So what? You can't live without shoes either

✤ An Indian called Squanto helped the Pilgrims survive their first bitter winter. He taught them how to plant corn and saved them from starving to death. Super Sqaunto. Still, half of the Pilgrims died of cold and disease that winter.

If only we could eat shoes

✤ The Indians had spent years clearing the forests to plant corn and built villages. The Pilgrim Fathers moved onto that land, and then into the empty Indian villages – the natives had run away.

Oh…this'll do

They stole from the Indian grain stores. A Pilgrim wrote…

> *We marched to a place called Cornhill where we had found corn once before. We dug and found three baskets full and a bag of beans, which will be enough. It was with God's help that we found this corn.*

Worst of all, they robbed Indian graves…

> *We found a place like a grave. We decided to dig it up. We found a mat, a fine bow, bowls, dishes and trays. We took several of the prettiest things to carry away with us and covered up the body again.*

The trouble is, the Pilgrims brought some nasty little friends with them … diseases. The Indians had never met these diseases before, and their bodies weren't protected against them, so they were killed off by the million. Poor Squanto died from one of the plagues … super-spotty Squanto.

And the Indian deaths made it easy for the settlers to spread till they took over the continent. Grim pilgrims.

AMERICA, 17 JUNE 1775
BUNKER HILL BATTLE

In 1775, America was still ruled by King George III and the British. The Americans didn't like paying their taxes to a king and country they never saw, and a government they weren't allowed to vote for. Would you? So they rebelled.

In 1775, the rebels gathered their weapons. A British general set off to seize them. American hero Paul Revere rode to warn the rebels and the fighting began. In the first big battle, the British attacked the American rebels at Bunker Hill, near Boston.

Joseph Warren was a rebel leader who had sent Paul Revere on his famous ride. He escaped the first battle, when a bullet hit him in the wig. But his luck ran out at the battle of Bunker Hill.

As he went into battle, he cried…

I hope I shall die up to my knees in British blood!

He got half of his wish. He died.

A British officer spotted Warren and he knew him. Bad luck, Warren. An ordinary rebel may have been taken prisoner. A rebel leader had to be shot.

Warren had gone into battle with the rebels' secret spy report in his pocket. The British took the secret report and buried Warren. When I say 'buried', a British soldier said…

We stuffed the scoundrel Warren, with another rebel, into one hole

Rebel secrets were given away … all because Warren was daft enough to take the report into a battle.

Oh poo … I am such a numpty*

*not a direct quote

Ten months later the Americans wanted to dig up Warren's corpse and put it in a proper grave. How would they know the rotting body was Warren? Warren had false teeth, made by Paul Revere. Paul Revere looked at the false teeth in the skull and said…

Those are the teeth I made for Warren! This is definitely his body!

Warren had famous false teeth … and famous last words. Reports said when Warren was wounded he called out gallantly…

I am a dead man, fight on my brave fellows, and save your country!

BUT a lot of people saw Warren die. He was shot in the face and the bullet went into his brain. It is very tricky trying to say such famous last words with a hole in your face and a bullet in your brain!

The truth? Warren's famous last words were as false as his teeth!

Fight on my brave fellows, and save my reputation!*

*Also not a direct quote

DEATH OF CAPTAIN COOK

Brit explorer, Captain James Cook, sailed the southern seas three times and in the end it killed him.

In 1776, he sailed off to the South Pacific and came across Hawaii. At first the natives on Hawaii were friendly. They thought Cook was their god Lono. Cook and his crew sailed off after a month and the natives were pleased … gods come to visit, NOT to stay. Lono, god of peace sailed away and it was time for the god of war to take his turn.

Then Cook's ship's mast broke and he came BACK to Hawaii. The natives were NOT so pleased. After all, the god of war was ruling now. What happened next was not pretty.

✹ The Hawaiians stole one of Cook's precious rowing boats.

✹ Cook landed on the beach and tried to take the King of Hawaii hostage till he got his boat back.

✹ The Hawaiians attacked. Cook was clubbed on the head and stabbed to death.

✹ Cook was a god so the chiefs looked after his body. His guts were taken out. His corpse was baked and the flesh scraped off. The crew rescued some bones and buried them at sea.

Many people think Captain Cook 'discovered' Australia. But the Dutch were the first people from Europe to find it in 1606 – over 160 years before Cook arrived. Captain Cook DID claim the land for Britain. And Britain found a good use for it – a place to dump their convicts.

Of course the native Australians – Aborigines – had been there for about 40,000 years. The Aborigines of Tasmania lasted only another 60 years after the Brits arrived. They were killed off by disease or starvation. Some were even hunted like animals and many began to kill their own babies.

The last Tasmanian woman, Truganini, must have died cursing Cook's cruel convicts.

13 MAY 1787

FIRST CONVICT SHIPS SAIL TO AUSTRALIA

The Brits had to 'transport' their villains to the new land Captain Cook had 'discovered' ... Australia.

On 13 May 1787, 717 convicts were loaded onto ships and sailed off from Portsmouth. They had 210 soldiers to guard them.

The youngest villain was John Hudson, a nine-year-old chimney sweep. He must have felt a bit lost, poor kid! After all, there weren't a lot of chimneys in Australia in those days.

48 of the other convicts died on the journey – which may have been better than living in Australia.

Some were punished for bad behaviour with 300, 400 or 800 lashes on the back.

Children weren't supposed to be transported till they were 14 but younger ones like John Hudson were still being sent to Australia in the 1830s.

The oldest was Dorothy Handland, who had been a rag dealer back in England. Dorothy was 88 years old and it's amazing she lasted that journey of 36 weeks. Others were not so lucky.

The trip was usually four or five months l-o-n-g and convicts often died of disease.

Many were held in chains or behind bars for the whole journey.

One boy was sent to Australia at the age of six. It's said he could hardly talk properly.

A boy of 16 grew to hate his prison officer so much he attacked him with an axe. The officer's leg was so badly injured it had to be amputated. The boy was hanged.

But how could you punish really rotten convicts who kept breaking the law – sort of 'super-convicts'?

Send them to Tasmania – just dump the convicts on the island and let them wander round to live or die. These wandering criminals were known as 'Bushrangers' and they brought terror to the natives of Tasmania … the Aborigines. The bushrangers killed the Aborigines as if it were a game.

A witness reported…

One bushranger, known as Carrots, killed an Aborigine man. Then he seized the dead man's wife. He cut off the man's head and fastened it round the wife's neck. Then he drove the weeping woman off to his den to be his slave.

Terrible Tasmania.

PARIS, 27 JULY 1794

THE END OF THE TERROR IN THE FRENCH REVOLUTION

The American Revolution had shown people that a revolt can get rid of a king. The poor people of France hated their kings and queens. At last they decided to do something about it. They chopped off the heads of their king, queen and lords. Then they started on just about anybody who didn't agree with them. This was known as the 'Terror'.

The Terror was led by a weedy little man called Maximilien Robespierre. In the end, everyone was so scared of Robespierre that they ganged up on him and set off to arrest him and his gang of bullies.

But many people still liked their Robespierre. A huge mob of his loyal supporters marched to Robespierre's rescue on the night of 27 July 1794. And they failed. What went wrong?

It rained. It was lashing down. The gutters turned into rivers that tore up the cobblestones in the streets. Dogs were drowning, rats were jumping out of the flooded sewers. We all went home and the soldiers went back to camp.

A man called Merda went to arrest Robespierre and said…

I saw Robespierre in the middle of the room. I leapt at him and pointed a sword at his heart and cried, 'Surrender, you traitor!' He looked up and said, 'It is you who are the traitor. I will have you shot.' I reached for one of my pistols and fired. I meant to hit him in the chest but the bullet struck his chin and smashed his bottom jaw. He fell out of the chair.

Robespierre had sent hundreds to the guillotine. Now it was his bloodstained turn. Over 80 of Robespierre's supporters followed him for the chop.

✹ Robespierre's brother, Augustin, tried to escape by jumping from a window. He broke his leg and was caught.

CHOP!

✹ His friend Couthon fell down stairs in his effort to get away and gashed his forehead. He went to the guillotine bandaged, screaming and wetting himself.

CHOP!

✹ Another friend, Hanriot, was thrown out of a window – but survived because he fell on a rubbish heap. Soldiers found him and tore out one eye which was left hanging down his cheek. As he climbed onto the guillotine the following evening a spectator snatched the eye off.

CHOP!

✹ Robespierre was patched up by a doctor so he was still alive when he went to the guillotine. The executioner tore off the bandage and his jaw almost fell away. A witness said, 'he let out a groan like a dying tiger. Everyone in the square heard it.' It didn't hurt for long.

CHOP!

A woman screamed at Robespierre…

Go to your grave with the curses of the wives and mothers of France. Your death makes me drunk with happiness.

I HEARD THAT!

In many parts of France the leaders of the Terror were executed and after that, the worst of the Terror was over.

AMERICA, MARCH 3 1807

A BAN ON NEW SLAVES

By the 1600s, slavery had become big business. Africans were captured, sent in ships across the Atlantic and sold in America. This went on for 150 years. The USA decided to stop bringing in new slaves from 1 January 1808 ... but slave owners could keep the ones they had.

The trip from Africa to America was the most torturous tour you could imagine.

The trade with Brazil was the LAST to be banned, in 1888. By then over 15 million Africans had been sent across the Atlantic – over two million had died on the terrible trips.

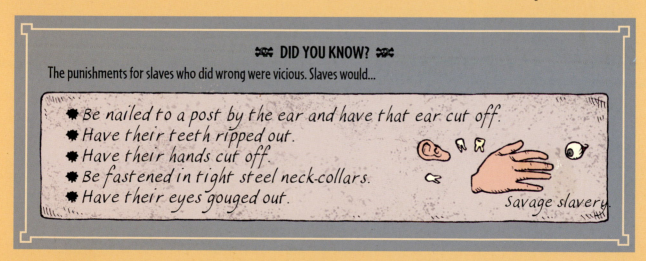

ENGLAND, 15 SEPTEMBER 1830
RAINHILL TRAIN ACCIDENT

In the late 1700s and 1800s, machines were invented that changed the world. This is known as the 'Industrial Revolution'. One of the greatest inventions was the steam train.

Some people said that if trains moved at over 40 miles an hour (64 kph), passengers in the open coaches would have the air sucked from their lungs and die. Queen Victoria had her own train. She refused to let it travel faster than 40 mph. That was potty.

But railways COULD be deadly. In 1821, David Brook, a carpenter in Leeds, crossed a train track in a sleet storm. He didn't see or hear the train and was knocked down. A fatal first. But Brook wasn't famous, so no one took much notice.

Most railway accidents in the 1820s were caused by exploding boilers – usually dead drivers and fried firemen. But they weren't famous either, so they were forgotten like Brook.

The first famous passenger to die was a Member of Parliament, William Huskisson. He was a guest at a railway race. A race to find the fastest locomotive in Britain. It took place at Rainhill near Liverpool. A witness told of the gory story…

> *The 'Northumbrian' locomotive pulled a carriage containing the Duke of Wellington. When it stopped the MP William Huskisson stepped down onto the track along which the 'Rocket' was seen rapidly coming up. The Duke of Wellington stretched out to shake the hand of Huskisson. A hurried, friendly grasp was given and, before it was loosed, there was a general cry of 'Get in! Get in!' Mr Huskisson, flustered, tried to get around the open door but in so doing was struck down by the 'Rocket'. His first words on being raised were, 'I have met my death!'*

Huskisson's leg was mangled. He was put in a carriage on the train that ran him down – the *Rocket*. They raced to get him to hospital but he died later that night.

The *Rocket* went on to win the speed trials by doing 29 mph (46 kph). But when it sped towards Manchester to save Huskisson's life it did the amazing speed of 36 mph (58 kph).

⚷⚷ DID YOU KNOW? ⚷⚷

One of the locomotives in the Rainhill Trials worked by horsepower. Real horsepower. Two horses walked along a treadmill that turned the wheels. The loco failed when one of the heavy horses crashed through the floor. Rein-hill failure.

IRELAND, 1845
POTATO FAMINE

Some of the world's worst disasters happen when food runs out and people starve to death ... a slow way to die. The Irish people were poor, but at least they could live on potatoes. Until 1845...

Planting potatoes was an easy way to live. You just planted your potatoes in April, picked them in August, and they could be stored and eaten until following May. Over summer your family had to buy oatmeal to eat. Some potatoes could be fed to your family pigs and they'd give you a bit of meat, but you had no savings to buy extra food because your landlord had to have his rent.

Then, in August 1845, a fungus attacked the potatoes and it spread quickly over the country. The potatoes looked all right, but when you pulled them up they were black and rotten inside.

These terrible true reports came from Ireland.

1 Lennox Biggar of Dundalk said... I tried boiling the potatoes in water. The smell was so bad I wouldn't even allow it to be fed to my pigs.

2 Asanath Nicholson went to Ireland to give out Bibles and she saw a curious sight... We found an island in Donegal deserted. All we could see were dogs. I wondered, 'How can the dogs look so fat and shining here, where there is no food for the people.' Then the pilot of my boat told me what dogs were eating: the corpses of the people.

3 Even the animals suffered, as an Irish woman reported: We ate the blood from a cow, baked with vegetables or anything we could find. Did you know that you could take two litres of blood from a living cow before it falls over?

4 And it wasn't just the cows... (Irish man): we ate the dogs first, then the donkeys, the horses, foxes, badgers, hedgehogs and even frogs. We stewed nettles and dandelions and collected all the nuts and berries we could find. The people on the coast could eat shellfish but a lot of them were poisonous. Maybe it was better a quick death from poisoning than a slow one from hunger.

5 There were even horror stories about the famine: (Irish woman) I was sent to look at the grave of Kate Barry. I saw what looked like the tail of a horse lying there. I lifted it and pulled up her skull   the hair was Kate Barry's and her grave had been so shallow the dogs had dug her up and eaten her.

The 1845 famine went on for four years. About a million people died. The Irish potato famine is history. But people around the world still starve to death every day.

MEERUT, 10 MAY 1857

INDIAN REBELLION

British ships and guns sailed around the world and invaded country after country. The Brits ended up with an empire greater than the ancient Roman Empire. And just as cruel.

Just like the Romans, the Brits robbed countries and got the defeated men to fight for them. But in India the Brits made a stupid mistake that cost thousands of lives.

Indian soldiers (called 'sepoys') were brilliant fighters, and the Brits used them all over the world. The Brits gave the sepoys new rifles with 'cartridges'. These cartridges had gunpowder under a paper cover. To load you had to …

1 Tear off the paper cover with your teeth.
2 Pour the gunpowder down the barrel.
3 Ram the cartridge with its bullet down the barrel.
4 Fire!

To help the bullet slide down (3), the cartridge was covered with grease. Of course, you'd get grease in your mouth when you bit off the paper cover (1).

The sepoys were not Christians like the Brit officers. They were mostly Hindu and Muslim. The Hindus were not allowed to touch cows (because they were sacred) and the Muslims were not allowed to touch pigs (because they were filthy). So it should have been simple for the Brits: 'Do NOT use grease made from the fat of cows OR pigs.' Easy!

What did the Brits do? They used grease made from the fat of cows AND pigs! Or so a rumour said. On 10 May 1857, the sepoys rebelled. Eighty-five soldiers refused to fire their rifles. They were marched off to prison. The next day, their friends started killing Brit officers as well as their wives and children. The rebels were set free and joined the killing.

Brit women and children were massacred…

Post 👑 Office

1857

✿ Five Brit men and 206 women and children were captured. The rebel leader, the Nana Sahib, decided to murder them all.

✿ The sepoy soldiers refused to execute the prisoners, so the Nana Sahib sent in butchers with axes and knives.

✿ The dead and dying were thrown into a deep well. When it was full, the rest were thrown into the river.

The Brit revenge was brutal…

Post 👑 Office

1857

✿ Muslim mutineers were sewn into PIG skins before they were hanged – a horror worse than death.

✿ Mutineers were forced to clean up the blood from the massacre – and if they refused they were lashed and made to lick it up.

✿ Indian rebels were hanged or tied to the mouth of a cannon and blown apart when the cannon was fired.

✿ At Jaunpur, rebel leaders were hanged from a tree then their bodies were shot at for sport.

✿ Indian women had to watch as their husbands and sons were hacked to death.

Two years later the war ended with the Brits back in control. Hundreds of Brit soldiers left the army when the mutiny was over. Were they shocked by the horrors? No. They had simply become filthy rich from all the loot they had stolen. They were the real winners.

JAMAICA

Jamaica, 11 October 1865
MORANT BAY REBELLION

BRITISH SLAVES IN JAMAICA WERE 'FREE' AFTER 1834 BUT THE OWNERS WERE STILL IN CONTROL. THE JAMAICANS HAD TO WORK FOR A PENNY A DAY.

In 1835, an angry mob of 500 ex-slaves marched on the town of Stony Gut armed with sticks, cutlasses, fishing spears and a few guns. The town guard turned out to face them. But who started the trouble? The women! The women had marched into town with their baskets full of stones and they began to throw them. When a stone hit the commander of the guard he ordered his men to open fire. The crowd rushed at them and began some murderous massacre…

* One soldier was killed with a harpoon.
* Rebels burned down the court-house with the judge inside.
* A Councillor, Baron Von Ketelhodt, was hacked to death and his fingers cut off by the rioters as prizes.
* It was said that the rebels cut out the tongue of preacher the Reverend Herschell while he was still alive, then tried to skin him.
* Lieutenant Hall was pushed into a burning building to roast alive.
* A Jamaican priest (but friend of the Brits) was beaten to death and his guts ripped out.

British Governor Edward Eyre said…

Many are said to have had their eyes scooped out, their heads split open and their brains taken out.

Governor's Eyre's revenge was terrible.

* One rebel called Wellington was shot and then had his head hacked off. The body was buried by a stream, but heavy rain swelled the stream and washed the head away. It was found and stuck on a pole.
* At Fonthill village nine men were shot then hung up in their local church.
* Over 600 were flogged – and the Brits often put strands of wire in the lashes to make them more painful.
* Jamaicans were hunted down and shot or hanged. Some were given trials and some weren't. A thousand homes were burned to the ground and 439 Jamaicans were killed.
* Men were lined up at a trench and shot so their bodies fell into the trench.

Governor Eyre was sacked, but he escaped real punishment.
Many Brits thought he was a hero.

USA, 15 APRIL 1865
ASSASSINATION OF PRESIDENT LINCOLN

In 1861, people of the USA started fighting each other. They had stopped bringing in new slaves in 1808, but the slaves that were already there stayed as slaves. The northern states wanted to set the slaves free. The southern states needed those slaves to pick cotton, so they said, 'No'.

In the end the North won. Northern leader President Abraham Lincoln became a hero. But the South had one nasty little surprise left … they couldn't kill all the people in the North but they COULD kill Lincoln. So a southerner did. A famous actor called John Wilkes Booth went to a theatre where Lincoln was watching a play. He crept up behind the president and shot him in the head. (Lincoln's bodyguard had gone off for a drink. Oooops.)

Americans LIKE to shoot their presidents. President John F Kennedy was shot in 1963 in Dallas. Some people have noticed strange things that link the killings. It is really rather creepy. But some of their 'facts' are not quite true. Which TWO of these ten 'facts' are lies?

1 Abraham Lincoln became President in 1860. John F. Kennedy became President in 1960.

2 Both presidents were shot in the head from behind.

3 Lincoln's secretary was named Kennedy. Kennedy's secretary was named Lincoln.

4 Both presidents were shot on a Friday while sitting next to their wives.

5 Both were assassinated by a man from a southern state.

6 Both were followed by a president named Johnson from the South. (Andrew Johnson, who followed Lincoln, was born in 1808. Lyndon Johnson, who followed Kennedy, was born in 1908.)

8 Both assassins were known by three names with 15 letters. (John Wilkes Booth, who assassinated Lincoln, was born in 1839. Lee Harvey Oswald, who shot Kennedy, was born in 1939.)

9 Lincoln was shot at the Ford theatre. Kennedy was shot in a Ford car.

10 Booth ran from the theatre and was caught in a warehouse. Oswald ran from a warehouse and was caught in a theatre. Booth and Oswald were both shot dead before they were sent to trial.

Fake facts? No one has proved Lincoln had a secretary called Kennedy (3) and Booth was born in 1838, not 1839 (6).

PARIS, 18 MARCH 1871
FRENCH COMMUNARD REVOLT

The French Revolution got rid of kings and queens in the 1790s. But 80 years later the people of Paris rose up against their Emperor. On 18 March 1871 they set up a rebel group and called themselves 'Communards'. The Communard revolt was nearly as horrible as the revolution. But in the end the Communards were crushed...

The ten foulest facts about the Communard revolt are...

1 The Communards surrounded a troop of government soldiers and dragged the leader, General Lecomte, from his horse. They took him to a house and shot him dead. The Communards were bad shots, so it took a lot of bullets.

2 Communard Police Chief Rigault was shot. His naked body was left in a gutter for two days to be kicked and spat on. His girlfriend finally covered it with a coat.

3 When the Communards executed the Bishop of Paris, they threw his body into a ditch by a cemetery to rot. In revenge, the Emperor's army took 147 Communards to the cemetery and shot them.

4 The Communard firing squads were clumsy. They took four policemen into a courtyard to be shot ... but hit just one of them. One escaped in the darkness. A man said they hunted him 'like a rat'.

5 A British doctor went to help in a Communard hospital. He was horrified to see the doctors use an instrument to pull bullets out of a wound then stir their coffee with the same instrument. Which is most horrible – the blood in the coffee or the coffee in the wounds?

6 A Communard general was killed with a sword blow that split his skull open. His corpse was loaded into a cart full of horse muck and taken back to the Emperor's camp. There, a witness said: 'Elegant ladies prodded the corpse's shattered skull with their umbrellas.'

7 Twenty-five women tried to defend their homes by pouring boiling water down on the heads of the Emperor's soldiers. They were captured and shot. The soldiers also searched for people with dirty, sooty hands because they believed they had been setting fire to the buildings; they found one man with really black hands and shot him dead on the spot. The poor man was an innocent chimney sweep.

8 A thousand Communards were rounded up and marched out of Paris to the Emperor's camp. Not all of them made it. An English witness said: 'Old men, women, girls and boys – some nearly in rags – were driven on by the horse-soldiers. I saw two soldiers guarding two young men. Suddenly the soldiers clubbed them down with the butt end of their rifles, placed a pistol in an ear of each one and pulled the trigger.'

9 The Emperor's commander, General Gallifet, told his soldiers: 'Shoot anyone wearing a watch – since these people are probably officers of the Communards. And shoot anyone who is unusually ugly or anyone with grey hair.'

10 When the Communards realized it was all over they took their prisoners out of their cells and shot them. Later a body was found with 69 bullets in it. Another had been stabbed with a bayonet 70 times. That's what you call hatred.

AFRICA, 1879
BATTLE OF ISANDLWANA

South Africa was rich in gold and diamonds so an army from Britain set out to get them. But they came up against the Zulu warrior tribes.

Lord Chelmsford arrived in South Africa with a British army. He soon started to squabble with the native Zulu king Cetshwayo. A band of 1,800 British troops marched into Zululand to sort out the Zulu king. The troops marched to the beat of drums, played by little drummer boys.

The two armies met at a rocky hill called Isandlwana.

- 🌸 The mass of Zulus rushed at the British so the Brits didn't have much chance to use their guns.
- 🌸 An eclipse of the sun turned the battlefield dark.
- 🌸 The Zulus stabbed at everything – even the cattle the Brits kept for food – crying, 'This is a gift to the spirits'.
- 🌸 Some Brits tried to escape on horseback but were caught in the swampy river, stabbed or drowned.
- 🌸 The ones in dark coats escaped. Cetshwayo only told his Zulus to kill the ones in red coats.
- 🌸 The horses were killed because Cetshwayo didn't want them. Even the British dogs were killed.
- 🌸 Many Brit soldiers were scalped, beheaded or gutted. It was a Zulu custom, not cruelty.

We rip open their bodies to set their spirits free so they can go to heaven.

One Zulu wrote about the battlefield years later:

The green grass was red with the running blood and the paths were slippery, for they were covered with the brains and entrails of the killed.

Most horrible of all the drummer boys were caught, hung up and chopped into pieces like meat in a butcher's shop.

It was the worst British defeat EVER against a native army. Back in Queen Victoria's Britain the people were shocked … especially by the horror of the drummer boys. They wanted just one thing … revenge.

The Brits came back with a stronger force, defeated the Zulus and captured Cetshwayo. It was the end of the Zulu kingdom.

🕸 DID YOU KNOW? 🕸

The British soldiers at Isandlwana had plenty of bullets. They were in wooden boxes with the lids screwed down. But they couldn't get them out – nobody had packed a screwdriver.

TSAR ALEXANDER II KILLED

The 1800s were a time of rotten revolts all over Europe. Rulers faced bullets and bombs and burnings and bricks. But in Russia the people REALLY wanted to kill their ruler, Tsar Alexander II. He faced more assassins than any other leader.

When Tsar Alex took the throne, Russia still had 30 million 'serfs' – peasants who could be bought or sold and were little more than slaves. He gave them their freedom, but still the rebels weren't happy. They shot at him in his royal palace, in his royal train and in his royal carriage, but missed (although they DID manage to kill a horse that got in the way). They tried to bomb him in his dining room – but only managed to kill soldiers and servants.

'ONLY SERVANTS AND SOLDIERS' THAT'S NICE

Finally the rebels, who called themselves 'Anarchists', came up with a double-bomb plot...

In March 1881, the commander of Alex's guards warned him, 'Don't go to the army parade tomorrow. It's too dangerous.'

Alex ignored the advice and set off in his carriage. On his way home he drove past crowds of people in the streets. A woman waved a handkerchief — the Tsar waved back, but she was actually waving a signal to her Anarchist friends.

A man ran from the crowd and threw a bundle, wrapped in a newspaper, under the horses' feet where it exploded in a cloud of smoke and snow. Why kill horses? Wait and see...

When the snow settled it was stained with the blood of two horses, two guards and an innocent butcher's boy who'd been watching the Tsar ride past.

But Tsar Alex wasn't hurt. His carriage windows were shattered but he was unharmed. He wanted to speak to the injured. Someone in the crowd called out...

ARE YOU HURT, YOUR MAJESTY?

NOT AT ALL THANK GOD

DON'T THANK GOD TOO SOON

That's when the second bomber stepped from the crowd and said...

He threw a second bomb at the Tsar. The horse bomb had been a plot to get him out of his carriage.

Bomb two tore gaping wounds in Alex's legs and chest. Alex struggled to his feet and managed to say...

TAKE ME HOME TO THE PALACE TO DIE

Take him home is what his guards did — and die is what Alexander II did a few hours later.

Alex's son took over, and his dead Dad's plan to give Russians the vote was scrapped. The rebels got themselves a worse life, not a better one. Of course Alex had no life at all. Neither had the butcher's boy. Or the horses.

But Russia hadn't finished with tslaying its tsars, as you'll see...

NORTH AMERICA, 29 DECEMBER 1890
BATTLE OF WOUNDED KNEE

The US settlers discovered gold in the west of America in 1849. Hundreds of families crossed America to make their fortunes. But they had to cross Native American Indian land ... and the Indians started to fight back.

The Sioux Indians used to roam across the plains of North America, killing buffalo with bows and arrows. Then along came settlers from Europe with guns. The buffalo were killed off, and the Indians were forced to live in small patches of poor land called 'reservations'. If they strayed or rebelled, they were killed by the United States Cavalry.

But then along came a Sioux 'shaman' (priest) called Wovoka. He said he could see into the future and he told Chief Big Foot's people…

The Ghost Dances spread across the Sioux people. The US settlers were scared of an Indian revolt. They sent in the army to force the Sioux back to a reservation at a place called Wounded Knee. Most of the warriors had handed over their rifles quietly – they were starving and too weak to put up a fight. The shooting started by accident…

- A soldier tried to take a rifle from a Sioux called Black Coyote. But he was deaf, and didn't understand, so he struggled. The rifle went off. The warriors feared they'd be shot so ran to get back their rifles.
- The soldiers started firing at the Sioux. Four army machine guns on the hillside fired at the Sioux tents.
- The tents were full of women and children. As the families ran for cover they were gunned down.
- One hundred and fifty-three Sioux died – half of them women and children. Over a hundred may have escaped but many of them died from the mid-winter cold. The magical Ghost Shirts didn't stop the bullets.
- Twenty-five soldiers died. But the soldiers were firing so wildly they probably shot one another.
- The US army gave out medals to the killers at Wounded Knee. They gave out more medals in this battle than in any other battle in US history. Medals for killing women and children?

China, 1 November 1897
BOXER REBELLION

China was another country where the armies of Europe went to war to win wealth. After years of suffering the Chinese decided to rebel.

A secret rebel group was set up – they called themselves 'The Society of the Righteous and Harmonious Fists' ... or 'Boxers'. They wore red ribbons round their heads and their wrists. (So not all THAT secret then.)

The Boxers invented a martial art that was so magical they could kill without being killed – just like the Ghost Dancing Indians. (In case their martial arts didn't work, they had swords and guns too.)

The Boxers wanted to change their country. Their simple idea was…

The first to go were the Christian missionaries from Europe – on 1 November 1897 two priests from Europe were killed. Then a Roman Catholic bishop was burned alive. They were the first of 30,000 to be killed.

Of course, the governments of Europe were angry. They wrote to Empress Cixi, the selfish and ignorant old empress who ruled China, and said: 'What are you going to do about it?'

The simple woman's simple reply was, 'Kill all foreigners!'

Yes, the Empress had swapped sides to help the rebels. (If she hadn't they may have killed her. Maybe she wasn't so daft after all.)

The armies of Europe landed in China with machine guns and the Boxers discovered their magic power didn't seem to stop bullets. End of rebellion … and end of empress.

But that wasn't good enough for the German emperor Wilhelm. He took an army of 30,000 to China, and told his troops…

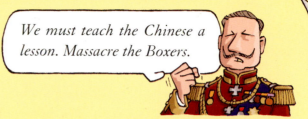

German General Waldersee wanted to show his emperor he could be the most savage soldier ever. In every village he took the head man out and shot him … in his head man head. Then it turned nasty. A Chinese leader ripped the skin off the German Baron Clemens von Ketteler and ate his heart.

What a heartless way to fight a war, eh?

ENGLISH CHANNEL, 25 JULY 1909
BLERIOT'S FLIGHT

Human beings have come up with some brilliant inventions. But sooner or later someone really brave has to try them out to see if they are safe for the rest of us.

Louis Bleriot is famous for being the first person to fly across water. He flew from France to England and his name went down in history. It was the most famous French landing since William the Conqueror landed at Hastings in 1066. But Bleriot should NOT have won the race to be first. He was just plain lucky.

❈ Bleriot was an engineer who had made his fortune inventing gas headlamps for cars

I WAS A REAL BRIGHT SPARK

❈ He then spent his money trying to make a flying machine. In 1900, he had built an ornithopter – an aircraft that flies by flapping its wings.

THAT IDEA DIDN'T GET OFF THR GROUND

NO, REALLY DIDN'T GET OFF THE GROUND

❈ He went on building dangerous, useless machines. At last he got the *Bleriot 5* plane in the air but it soon crashed. A bit of a nuisance. Just as he finished building the *Bleriot 9* the *Daily Mail* newspaper announced a contest.

£1000 prize for the first pilot to fly across the English Channel

❈ Bleriot needed the money so he entered the race … but he had a great rival: Henry Latham, a filthy-rich Frenchman. Henry's *Antoinette* plane had broken records and won prizes in Europe and America – it was top favourite to win the *Mail's* money.

❀ Latham set off a week before Bleriot was ready. But his engine failed and Latham became the first man to make a landing at sea. The rescuers found him sitting calmly in his plane, smoking a cigarette. He was just six miles short of the English coast.

❀ Bleriot had a second chance. But Latham had a new machine ready. He told Bleriot…

> TELL YOU WHAT, MON AMI, LET'S MAKE IT A RACE. WE'LL SET OFF AT DAWN ON 25 JULY

> IT'S A DEAL

❀ But disaster struck. As Bleriot was testing his *XI* machine a fuel line split, a fire broke out and his foot was burned. He bravely agreed to carry on. It was his third and final chance. At first light on 25 July 1909, Bleriot soared into history as he flew the 22 miles in 37 minutes.

Rain, strong winds and mist failed to beat him. He was a hero of history around the world.

BUT … 'What happened to Latham?' you cry. If I tell you, you won't believe it. Have a guess…

a) He crashed into the sea … again.

b) He crashed into a seagull and smashed his propeller. (The seagull was a bit smashed too.)

c) His servant forgot to set the alarm clock so he was still asleep when dawn broke.

Answer (c) The servant forgot to wake him. Latham slept in. He wasn't ready to fly at dawn. That's how history is made.

Antarctic, 29 March 1912
DEATH OF CAPTAIN SCOTT

Men didn't just race for prizes. They raced for pride – even if it killed them. Brit Captain Robert Scott was in a bit of race against Roald Amundsen from Norway. Each wanted to be the first man to reach the South Pole. The trouble is it's very cold and very snowy there, and there aren't any shops around when you run out of food.

Captain Scott first set sail for the South Pole in 1901. Our Horrible Histories reporter was with him.

Scott was sure he could reach the South Pole so he went home to Britain to make a bigger and better plan. Back in Britain he was a hero. He told everyone that he would get to the Pole for Britain and the Empire. In 1910, he set off again…

Pitiful ponies were useless. Ponies needed to carry a huge haystack of food for themselves. Their hooves broke through the ice. Scott's men had to do the walking and the pulling.

Scott and his team of four reached the Pole on 17 January 1912 … but he found Amundsen had beaten them by five weeks.

Captain Scott and the four others set off on the 800-mile trip back. They didn't make it. But his diary did. It shows how upset he was at losing.

The worst has happened. All day-dreams must go. Great God! This is an awful place

One by one they fell. Edgar Evans fell and died of the cold. Lawrence Oates limped along with an old war wound. He knew he was holding the others back so he walked off into the snow saying the famous last words…

I am just going outside and may be some time.

Twenty miles further on, the snows swallowed the last two in the team, and they died. Scott wrote…

Our dead bodies must tell the tale

The British people made Scott a hero. They tried to make out the real hero, Amundsen, was a bit of a sneaky cheat!

The Brits were BAD losers.

ATLANTIC OCEAN, 14 APRIL 1912
THE *TITANIC* SINKS

1912 was not a good year for humans to go into battle with ice. Scott lost his battle in Antarctica. Just two weeks later 1,500 more lost their lives in an icy ocean. If you build a ship, then boast it is 'unsinkable', you just know what will happen next.

1 THE *TITANIC* LAUNCHED IN BELFAST, IRELAND, IN 1911 AND WHEN IT HIT THE WATER IT SUCKED SMALLER SHIPS TOWARDS IT AND ALMOST CRASHED.

EEK

IT'S A DISASTER WAITING TO HAPPEN

2 THERE WERE ENOUGH LIFEBOATS FOR 1,178 PEOPLE ... BUT THE SHIP SET SAIL FROM ENGLAND TO THE USA WITH 2,240 PEOPLE ON BOARD.

OOOPS! JUST HAVE TO HOPE SHE DOESN'T SINK. HEH! HEH!

3 ON THE NIGHT OF SUNDAY, 14 APRIL 1912 IT WAS FREEZING. SHIPS SENT RADIO MESSAGES WARNING ABOUT ICEBERGS. BUT THE CREW OF THE *TITANIC* DIDN'T TELL THE CAPTAIN.

ALL THE POSH PEOPLE ON THE SHIP WANTED TO HEAR THEIR MESSAGES FROM HOME

WELL, I PAID A LOT FOR THIS TRIP

4 JUST BEFORE MIDNIGHT, AN ICEBERG TORE THROUGH THE SIDE OF THE SHIP AND SHE BEGAN TO SINK. THE CAPTAIN GAVE THE ORDER TO ABANDON SHIP.

WOMEN AND CHILDREN FIRST!

LEND ME YOUR WIG AND YOUR DRESS DARLING

5 MOST OF THE POSH PASSENGERS LIVED ... MOST OF THE POOR PASSENGERS DIED.

I PAID FOR IT

BUT THE POOR PAID A HIGHER PRICE ... IT WAS A BUSY NIGHT FOR DEATH

The chief builder of *Titanic* was Thomas Andrews. It was Andrews who said…

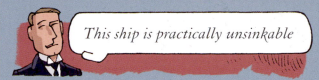

This ship is practically unsinkable

Andrews was on the *Titanic* when it hit the iceberg. He helped passengers into the lifeboats, and then went down into one of the posh rooms and threw off his life jacket.

One of the crew asked, 'Aren't you even going to try to save yourself, sir?' Andrews didn't reply. He went down with his practically unsinkable ship.

Only 706 passengers survived that night – 1,517 died. The story of a man who dressed as a woman – so he could get on a lifeboat – is probably true. He was Bruce Ismay, president of the company that owned *Titanic*. Two dogs lived to tell the tale, too.

GOOD THING I'M A POSH DOG

YAP YAH

FLANDERS, 1918
FIRST WORLD WAR

By 1914, machine guns were able to fire a hail of bullets and millions began to die in the worst war history had seen. Yet just ONE bullet could have saved another 50 million lives. ONE bullet that WASN'T fired. It's one of the strangest tales in all of horrible history...

Private Henry Tandey was fighting in the First World War. He set off to attack a German trench. Suddenly a wounded German soldier limped out of the enemy trench and into Private Tandey's line of fire.

The exhausted German never raised his rifle and just stared at Tandey waiting to be shot. Tandey said...

I took aim but I couldn't shoot a wounded man, so I let him go.

The young German soldier nodded in thanks and ran off to safety.

If Tandey had moved his finger a centimetre and pulled the trigger, the German would have died and history would have changed. The German soldier's name was Adolf Hitler.

Hitler went on to lead the German people into the Second World War. At least 50 million people died in that war.

And all because a British soldier didn't move his finger one centimetre.

Twenty years later Adolf Hitler later asked the British Prime Minister to thank Henry Tandey for saving his life. Hitler then went to war with Britain. During the war he sent bombers to flatten the city of Coventry. Tandey was living in Coventry at the time and escaped the bombs by sheltering in a doorway. He later said...

If only I had known what Hitler would turn out to be. When I saw all the people, woman and children he had killed and wounded I was sorry to God I let him go.

Tandey lived through the Coventry bombing. Millions of other died from Hitler's horrors.

YEKATERINBURG, RUSSIA, 17 JULY 1918
RUSSIAN ROYAL FAMILY KILLED

During the First World War (1914-1918), the Russians were doing badly. Tsar Nicholas II took command of the army himself ... and things just got worse. The Russians blamed Nick, so they had a revolution and the 'Communist' rebels took over the country. Nick had to give up the throne.

The Tsar and his family were sent to Ipatiev House in Yekaterinburg. There was an army of friends on the way to rescue them, so the rebels decided the royal family had to die ... all of them.

But massacres can be messy. The royal family were woken up, told to dress, and taken to the basement.

There may be some shooting, we don't want you to get hurt

The first part is true ... the second part isn't

Nicholas had his wife Alexandra with him, as well as their children, their doctor, and three of their servants.

The firing squad of seven entered the room, and their commander said the Tsar was sentenced to death. Nicholas cried out...

WHAT? WHAT?

The soldiers pulled out pistols and the killing began. Nicholas was the first to die.

❧ His daughters Anastasia, Tatiana, Olga, and Maria lived through the first hail of bullets; the bullets bounced off the 1.3 kilos of jewels that were sewn into their clothes. So they were stabbed with bayonets and then shot at close range in the head.

❧ Their skeletons were found thrown together under a road 80 years later. The Communists finally lost power in 1991. The new president, Boris Yeltsin, had Ipatiev House destroyed.

The murdered family was finally given a proper burial in 1998.

USA, 14 FEBRUARY 1929
ST VALENTINE'S DAY MASSACRE

People can be awkward. Tell them they MUST NOT do something and suddenly they WANT to do it. In the USA in the 1920s the people were told 'You must not drink alcohol'. So, of course, they found ways to beat the ban.

The ban on drinking was known as 'Prohibition'. As soon as booze was banned on 17 January 1920 people tried to make it and sell it without the police finding out. Some made a fortune. But they had to protect the money with gangs of violent men. One of the most vicious gang leaders was Big Al Capone who sold booze in Chicago. And it didn't pay to upset Big Al…

One man who tried to steal Capone's business was 'Bugs' Moran. Al Capone set up a very special Valentine's Day gift for 'Bugs', then Al went on holiday to Florida.

The amazing thing about the story was the way it appeared in the newspapers the next day!

 # Chicago Herald

15 February 1929

COPS CHOP BUGS BOYS

Last night seven members of the Bugs Moran gang died in a hail of machine-gun bullets. On St Valentine's Day, last night, the men arrived at a warehouse in Clarke Street to wait for a truckload of stolen whiskey. But there was no whiskey – only death in a police trap.

A local man, Andy Reiss, described the scene: 'I heard a truck door slam and looked out of my window opposite the warehouse.

I saw two cops in uniform and two plain-clothes detectives get out of a police wagon. They ran into the warehouse. That's when I heard a sound like a pneumatic drill – I guess that was the machine gun! Then the two uniformed cops came out with their guns pointed at two other men. It all went quiet for a while then we heard the guard dog begin to howl. It didn't stop so we went across to look.'

SLAUGHTERHOUSE

Reiss's neighbour (who did not wish to give his name) said, 'The door was open so we went in. It was like a slaughterhouse in there. There were seven bodies. The cops had just lined them up against the wall and blasted them. The blood was flooding over the floor and into the drain. The only sound was one guy moaning. We went and called for an ambulance but it was too late for him. It's a bit of a shock to think the police can murder men in cold blood like that!'

The neighbour's wife added, 'Moran's gang stole booze from a police gang two weeks ago. Bet ya this was their revenge!'

POLICE DENY INVOLVEMENT

The police chief denies that Chicago police force had anything to do with the massacre.

Our reporter tracked down 'Bugs' Moran at his home today. Moran agreed the dead men were members of his gang but insisted, 'That was meant to be me in there. I stopped off for a cup of coffee so I was late. I saw the police run in and I escaped with my life. But I thought it was just an ordinary raid! I just can't believe the police would do this to my boys. We pay the cops too well. Only Capone kills like that!' The investigation continues.

The newspapers got some of the facts right but one important one wrong … the killers were NOT the Chicago police. They were Al Capone's gang dressed up as police. They fooled their victims who lined up against the wall to be searched, and they fooled the witnesses.

The four killers were never punished for the St Valentine's Day massacre, but two died horribly anyway. These two, Anesimi and Scalise, agreed to turn in their boss, Al Capone. Big Al heard about their plot and planned a suitable revenge.

Capone arranged a dinner party where Anesimi and Scalise were the main guests. Al gave a speech and talked about how important it was to be loyal to your boss. Then he had Anesimi and Scalise tied to their chairs. He took out a baseball bat and, in front of his guests, battered the heads of the traitors till they were dead.

So prohibition was an awful idea. It led to gangsters and murder. The laws were scrapped on 23 March 1933 … but the lawless gangsters went on.

GERMANY, 9 NOVEMBER 1938
KRISTALLNACHT

Germany was in a mess after being beaten in the First World War. Along came a young man called Adolf Hitler who said he would sort it out ... if the people gave him power.

He was made leader of the Nazi party and he gathered a gang of about 15,000 bully boys – storm troopers in brown shirts.

Adolf Hitler said the Jews in Germany were to blame for them losing the war. In Paris a young Jew bought a gun and shot one of Hitler's men. That was just the excuse the Nazis needed to start destroying Jews in Germany.

On 9 November 1938, Hitler sent his storm troopers to punish the Jews. The bullies…

❁ Smashed the windows of Jewish shops, homes and prayer houses (synagogues). That's why it is known as 'Kristallnacht' – 'crystal-night', or 'the night of broken glass'.
❁ Arrested healthy young Jewish men and sent them to work in concentration camps.
❁ Burned down the homes of ordinary Jewish people .
❁ Beat men, women and children as they ran into the streets, and robbed their homes.
❁ Attacked Jewish cemeteries and tore down gravestones.

Many German people hated what they saw but couldn't stop Hitler's thugs. Other Germans came onto the streets and cheered the storm troopers – they held up their babies to watch the 'fun'. They even forced the Jews to scrub the pavements.

The men in the concentration camps suffered torture and beating. A Brit newspaper reported on one group of 62 Jewish prisoners who were beaten until they dropped, then beaten again …

> *By the end, twelve of the 62 were dead, their skulls smashed. The others were all unconscious. The eyes of some had been knocked out, their faces flattened and shapeless.*

The Nazis said the Jews were a problem. They came up with a 'Final Solution' … kill them ALL. Six million died horribly in the next six years … but it all started with Kristallnacht.

POLAND, 3 SEPTEMBER 1941
AUSCHWITZ

History has always been horrible. But in many ways it has become worse. The more humans invent clever things, the more the clever things can be used to murder people.

Hitler had some crazy ideas. Dreadful and deadly ideas. He thought the people of northern Europe were the best and should rule the world. Other people – 'under-humans' – could be slaves, or die. And to help them die, he had a gas called Zyklon B…

ZYKLON B'S TERRIBLE TIMETABLE

1918 Dr Fritz Haber wins the famous Nobel Prize for his clever work developing artificial fertilizers. He also invents poison gases in the First World War – he is even on the battlefield to help release the gases. His wife Clara hates his work so much she shoots herself.

1920s The gas Zyklon B is invented by Dr Fritz Haber's company to kill insects like lice that crawl through clothes.

1933 The Nazis start to attack Jews in Germany. Dr Haber is a Jew. Even though he is a German poison-gas hero he runs away to Switzerland and dies.

1939 The Second World War starts. The Nazis want to see if Zyklon B will kill people quickly. They test it on some mentally ill patients to see how well it works.

1940 The Nazis start to fill up their concentration camps with Jews, gypsies, beggars, tramps and criminals. They test the gas on 250 gypsy CHILDREN in the Buchenwald concentration camp

3 September 1941 The real mass killing begins. In June 575 sick prisoners are gassed with Zyklon B at Auschwitz camp. They are too ill to work and too useless to feed.

January 1942 The top Nazis come up with a plan to get rid of the Jews completely by executing them all. They call it the 'Final Solution' – kill 11 million Jews. New death camps are built.

April 1942 Now Jews, Russian soldiers and sick prisoners are being sent to be executed – 2,000 at a time in Auschwitz. Pellets of Zyklon B are dropped into the death chambers. Those inside die in 20 minutes. Nazi doctor Johann Kremer said…

Shouting and screaming of the victims could be heard through the opening and it was clear that they fought for their lives.

Zyklon B's inventor, Dr Fritz Haber, was dead by the time his gas was used against the Jews in Europe.

But his Jewish family was not. Haber's relatives were among the six million Jews who died in the death camps. Some died from disease, cold, bullets and torture. Many died from Haber's gas.

And that is probably the horriblest history of all.

INTERESTING INDEX